# Vineyard
# CUISINE

# Vineyard CUISINE

### Meals & Memories from Messina Hof

## Merrill & Paul Bonarrigo

BRIGHT SKY PRESS

BRIGHT SKY PRESS

Box 416
Albany, Texas 76430

10   9   8   7   6   5   4   3   2   1

Library of Congress Cataloging-in-Publication Data

Bonarrigo, Merrill, 1952–
    Vineyard cuisine : meals and memories from Messina Hof /
    by Merrill and Paul Bonarrigo.
        p. cm.
    Includes index.
    ISBN 978-1-933979-02-1 (jacketed hardcover : alk. paper)  1.  Cookery
(Wine)  2.  Messina Hof Winery & Resort.  3.  Wine and wine making—
Texas.  I.  Bonarrigo, Paul, 1947–  II. Messina Hof Winery & Resort.  III.
Title.

TX726.B56 2007
641.6'22—dc22
                                                         2007007714

Book and cover design by Isabel Lasater Hernandez
Edited by Kristine Krueger


Printed in China through Asia Pacific Offset

*Gratefully Yours, Paul and Merrill*

To the Lord who has been so gracious to us, and to our family and friends who have encouraged and supported us over the years, we thank you for your love and faith that propelled us to pursue the dream we know as Messina Hof.

We are grateful to have had you as part of our family and to have shared this extraordinary experience.

Life is a journey. Every day is a gift to be cultivated and savored.

*"This is the day that the Lord has made, let us rejoice and be glad in it."*
*(Psalm 118:24 NIV)*

# The Birth of a Texas Vineyard

The Texas wine industry was born in 1560, when Spaniards pioneered Texas, brought vines and planted them at missions, believing the vines would prosper. In the late 1800s, T.V. Munson believed that Texas rootstock would save the French viticulture industry, and it did. In the 1970s, a group of pioneers believed that quality wine grapes would grow in Texas.

Pioneers see beyond limitations of human viewpoint with a faith that something yet unseen can and does exist. Pioneers believe and are willing to take the leap of faith to act as guide for those who do not.

Paul Bonarrigo was a pioneer. He grew up in the Bronx, where people stayed with the family and did the same things the generation before them did. He was the first in his family to get a college education, and from Columbia University at that. He was the first in the neighborhood to bring back a non-Sicilian wife.

Pioneering was not alien to me, either. I had been in one of the first classes of women at Texas A&M University, graduating in business administration, and accustomed to frontiers where women were not readily welcomed. So when I—a blond German Protestant from Texas—stood on the front porch of Paul's grandmother's home in a purely Sicilian Catholic New York neighborhood, it was just another frontier.

Perhaps it took two such pioneers to give birth to a vineyard and winery in Texas ... or was it just two silly, carefree, stubborn kids fulfilling a plan that only they could see? I do believe that all things happen for a reason.

On a spring day in 1977, two very different people saw a vision that one plus one could become much more if they took what was good in each and amplified its importance to a relationship. The Lord had a plan for us. We just needed to open our hearts to His plan.

*"According to your faith will it be done to you." Matthew 9:29 (NIV)*

—*Merrill Bonarrigo*
*Bryan, Texas*
*Spring 2007*

# Recipes From Our Roots

## A GERMAN-ITALIAN LOVE STORY

Charles and Georgia Mitchell raised two girls, Merrill Ann and Monie Sue, in Bryan, Texas, with the philosophy that they wanted their children to have a better life. They taught us we could do anything we chose to do and that with God, all things are possible.

Paul and Rose Bonarrigo raised a son and daughter, Paul and Rose, in the Bronx, New York, with that same philosophy.

My dream was to have a bakery and to own land. Growing up, I did all the baking for my family, and from a very early age I decided I would own the "Ponderosa" (*Bonanza* was my favorite television show). A family friend who was a tax accountant owned a great deal of land. He told me that he had acquired the land by assuming the tax burden in exchange for ownership. Right then, I decided I would become a tax accountant in order to acquire my Ponderosa. After one semester in accounting at Texas A&M University, I realized my personality was in sales, not in ledger sheets. So I pursued real estate as my profession.

At the same time, Paul was attending Edward H. Bryan School in New Jersey, playing sports and singing in a band. After graduation from Columbia University, he entered the medical service corps of the U.S. Navy. During the Vietnam War, Americans in some parts of the country were not supportive of our troops. But that wasn't what Paul found on a trip through Texas. —*Merrill*

While I was stationed in Oakland, California, I took care of the returning wounded. On days off, I attended classes at UC Davis and the Napa Wine School, where I learned the technical aspects of winemaking.

During that time, I participated in a harvest at Beaulieu Vineyard. Later, when having dinner at the Fairmont Hotel in San Francisco, I requested a bottle of the George de Latour Private Reserve, the most prized wine at the time. The incredulous response I got was that the Fairmont only served "fine" wines from France, Italy, Spain and Germany. California wines were not considered good enough to be on the wine list. Years later, this experience would ring in my head as I relived it with Texas wines.

As I drove from Oakland to Pensacola, Florida, for a change in duty stations, I stopped at a diner in West Texas. After I'd finished eating and was ready to leave, I asked the owner for the bill. He put his hand on my shoulder and told me the meal was on the house in thanks for my military service to America. Then when I asked if he could recommend a place to stay, the owner referred me to a motel where the room was free for military personnel.

Nowhere had I been so warmly welcomed or appreciated. I told myself that if Texas was full of those kind of people, that is where I want to live.

Then in 1971, the Lord used physical therapy to bring me back to Texas and more importantly to Bryan, Texas, where I would meet the love of my life. —*Paul*

# It All Began with a House Showing and a Precocious Pet ...

In 1975, I had a client who wanted to buy a contemporary house. As a Realtor in the quickly developing community of Bryan-College Station, Texas, I got calls all the time. The unique issue about this call was that the couple was from California wine country and wanted a contemporary home. I found three. Only one expressed an interest in securing a listing. His name was Paul Bonarrigo.

Paul was very cordial on the phone; his voice reminded me of a nice family doctor. During the initial tour of the house, Paul explained that the only thing I'd need to do in order to show the house was to get his dog, a very precocious boxer, into the garage before my client rang the doorbell. "Sonny" had a "different" way of greeting guests. He crouched in the kitchen and charged the full

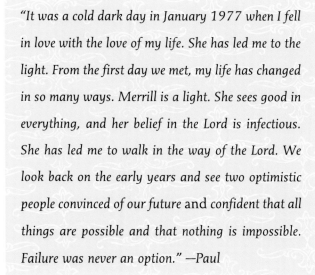

*"It was a cold dark day in January 1977 when I fell in love with the love of my life. She has led me to the light. From the first day we met, my life has changed in so many ways. Merrill is a light. She sees good in everything, and her belief in the Lord is infectious. She has led me to walk in the way of the Lord. We look back on the early years and see two optimistic people convinced of our future and confident that all things are possible and that nothing is impossible. Failure was never an option." —Paul*

length of the house to the door. As soon as Sonny came within leaping distance, he physically threw his body against the door while howling. This, it seems, was his way of warding off unwanted visitors. Paul assured me that by throwing a dog biscuit into the garage, Sonny would follow the biscuit, allowing me to close the door behind him.

The day of the showing, I went early to make sure everything was ready, started the coffeepot and put some of my fresh cinnamon rolls in the oven. These rolls were a family tradition for our Christmas morning breakfasts. If all else failed, these rolls always sealed the deal!

15

Sonny had been watching me quietly. Ten minutes prior to the arrival of my clients, I retrieved the dog biscuits from the pantry. Shaking the box so Sonny could see and hear them, I opened the garage door and threw in a biscuit. Sonny just sat there and looked at me. I showed him another and threw it into the garage. No luck. With a full box of biscuits piled on the garage floor, Sonny still sitting in the kitchen and my clients ready to arrive, I had to switch to plan B.

I grabbed Sonny's collar to hold him back. Just as I had control of his collar, the doorbell rang and off we went—Sonny in full stride and me riding him like a horse at the Kentucky Derby. Fortunately, the extra 100 pounds I added to Sonny's back prevented him from leaping into the door, though we hit the tile foyer at full speed and crashed into the door.

I assured my clients through the closed door that everything was okay, telling them the dog was under control and that they could come in. They declined politely and left. I never heard from them again. I never expected to hear from Paul again either.

Sonny, having completed his responsibilities of securing the premises, remembered the dog biscuits that were still in the garage and hurried off to finish them. I locked the door behind me and called Paul to let him know of the situation. I told him the clients had decided against the house and wished him the best.

Two years passed, then I received a call from Paul. The voice was familiar and I immediately recognized it as the gentle doctor's. He informed

me that he wished to sell his home. It would be easier this time because, sadly, Sonny had since passed away.

On January 28, I appraised the house and Paul took me to dinner that night. We talked for hours. By the end of dinner, it seemed we had known each other for years. —*Merrill*

*"When my grandmother found out that I had been dating Paul, she typed up a resumé for me and delivered it to his office. She said some of the ladies in her Sunday school class had been treated by Paul through physical therapy and highly recommended him as a husband. What a matchmaker!" —Merrill*

# Merrill's Cinnamon Rolls

*Dough*
¹/₃ cup milk
¹/₄ cup sugar, *divided*
¹/₂ teaspoon salt
¹/₄ cup butter, cubed
1 package (¹/₄ ounce) active dry yeast
¹/₄ cup warm water (110°)
1 egg
2¹/₂ cups unsifted all-purpose flour, *divided*

*Filling*
³/₄ cup butter, softened, *divided*
1 cup packed light brown sugar, *divided*
¹/₄ cup chopped pecans
¹/₂ cup pecan halves
¹/₂ cup chopped raisins, soaked in port overnight
¹/₂ teaspoon ground cinnamon

In a saucepan, heat milk just until it begins to bubble. Remove from the heat; add 2 tablespoons sugar, salt and butter; stir until butter is melted. Cool to lukewarm.

In a mixing bowl, sprinkle yeast and remaining sugar over warm water; stir until dissolved. Allow yeast to begin frothing. Add milk mixture, egg and 2 cups flour; beat until smooth. Add remaining flour; mix by hand until smooth.

Turn dough onto a lightly floured pastry cloth; knead until dough is smooth and blisters appear. Place in a large lightly greased bowl, turning once. Cover with a towel and let rise in a warm draft-free place until doubled.

Meanwhile, in small mixing bowl, cream ½ cup butter and ½ cup brown sugar. Spread onto the bottom and up the sides of a square baking pan. Sprinkle with chopped pecans.

On a lightly floured pastry board, roll dough into a 16-inch x 12-inch rectangle. Spread with remaining butter and sprinkle with remaining brown sugar; sprinkle with pecan halves, raisins and cinnamon. Roll up from a long side, jelly-roll style, and pinch seam to seal. Cut crosswise into 12 pieces. Place cut side down in prepared pan.

Cover and let rise in a warm draft-free place until doubled. Bake at 375° for 25–30 minutes or until golden. Invert pan onto a board and let stand for 1 minute. Remove rolls from pan.

Makes 1 dozen and sells a house

# Mini Potato Pancakes

3 medium potatoes, peeled and shredded
¼ cup chopped green onions
4 eggs
2½ tablespoons all-purpose flour
1 teaspoon minced garlic
½ teaspoon minced fresh thyme
½ teaspoon minced fresh Cuban oregano
¼ teaspoon salt
⅛ teaspoon black pepper
¼ cup olive oil
*Apple Topping*
1 apple, peeled, cored and thinly sliced
¼ cup slivered red onion
3 tablespoons olive oil
¼ cup Messina Hof Chenin Blanc
¼ cup packed brown sugar
2 tablespoons apple cider vinegar
1 tablespoon minced garlic
1 tablespoon butter

In a large bowl, combine the potatoes, green onions, eggs, flour, garlic, thyme, oregano, salt and pepper. Form into pancakes, about 3 inches in diameter. Heat oil on a griddle or in a skillet; fry pancakes until golden brown on both sides. Meanwhile, in a saucepan, cook apple and red onion in oil until apple is soft and onion is translucent. Add the remaining topping ingredients; cook until sugar is liquefied and mixture is bubbly. Serve with potato pancakes.

Serves 4

Georgia Mitchell with daughters Merrill and Monie

# Miniature German Rouladen

*We were married May 5, 1977 at my parents' home. In attendance were my parents, Charles Merrill and Georgia Mitchell; my grandmother, "Honey" Botting; my sister and her husband, Monie and Don Smith; and the pastor.*

*Though it was an intimate gathering on a Thursday after work, my mother used all of her many talents to create a beautiful altar and reception table. The menu was simple but elegant: Gulf Coast Shrimp cocktail, Italian meatballs in fresh tomato and basil sauce, and Miniature German Rouladen.*

1 pound veal cutlets (¹⁄₈ inch thick), tenderized
Dill gherkins
All-purpose flour
Oil for frying
Salt, pepper and dill weed to taste

Cut veal lengthwise into 2-inch-wide strips. Place a gherkin on each strip; roll up and secure with a toothpick. Dredge lightly in flour. Heat the oil in a skillet; fry roll-ups until golden brown (do not overcook, as veal will become tough). Drain on paper towels. Season with salt, pepper and dill.

Serves 6

# "Roots" Inspired Us to Research Ours

Fascinated by heritage and its importance in everyone's lives, Merrill and I researched our roots. Spurred on by the miniseries *Roots* by Alex Haley, which debuted the year of our marriage, we discovered my paternal family came from a small village called Gualtieri Sicomino in the mountains above Messina, Sicily. My dad was born in Gualtieri and came to America when he was 13.

My family had made wine in Sicily, and each winemaker was named Paul. My grandfather, Paul IV, had come to America in order to plant grapes in New York, by way of Philadelphia, but was deterred due to Prohibition. He became a cobbler and continued to make the family wine from grapes trucked into the neighborhood from California. My grandfather, father and I worked together to make each year's family wines.

I can still remember the aroma of fresh grapes as my grandfather selected the varieties off of the truck that would go into that vintage. Together we carried the crates of grapes through the neighborhood and down into the basement, where the magic of winemaking began. These early experiences were a foundation of my life. —*Paul*

My maternal family originated in Hof, Germany. My great-grandfather, Martin Kuno Sachs, left behind the Sachs bakery to become a brick maker in the United States. From Ellis Island, he traveled to Philadelphia (I wonder if Paul's grandfather and my great-grandfather ever met) to Fredericksburg,

Paul V and Mama Rosa

Texas, to Grapevine, Texas, and then to Houston, where he settled.

Martin had 12 children. My grandmother was the oldest girl and in charge of the other children. She was quite a woman. The grandchildren called her Honey. With two toddlers, Honey became a single mom during the Depression. She held down three jobs and rented out every room of her home, except the living room, where she and her babies stayed. She was never without a smile and never without hope.

In our three-generation home, Honey was definitely the spice of the house. My grandmother's faith was the strongest I have ever known, and my mother was also a strong Christian. Both my mother and father came from family backgrounds that did not believe in alcohol consumption. Paul and I were appreciative that they opened their hearts to our dream of Messina Hof.

Each of our forefathers left their homelands to pioneer a new land. Each brought family traditions and recipes from home, which we share in this chapter. —*Merrill*

# Venison Knishes with Mustard Sauce

*I had always thought of these as German fritters, until my first New York trip with Paul, when I tried potato knishes from a street vendor. They seemed to be on every corner, selling hot dogs, pretzels with mustard and more ... I had never seen so much food consumed on the run.*

2 cups venison sausage
½ cup finely diced green bell pepper
½ cup finely diced red bell pepper
¼ cup finely diced onion
1 teaspoon minced garlic
¼ cup veal stock
1 tablespoon hot pepper sauce
1 tablespoon Worcestershire sauce
1 teaspoon minced fresh thyme
½ teaspoon minced fresh Cuban oregano
½ teaspoon black caraway seed
Salt and pepper to taste
1 cup mashed potatoes
½ cup heavy whipping cream
¼ cup mustard of your choice
¼ cup all-purpose flour
Oil for frying

In a sauté pan, cook the sausage over high heat for 2 minutes; drain if necessary. Add peppers, onion and garlic; sauté until onions are translucent. Add the stock, hot pepper sauce, Worcestershire sauce, thyme, oregano, caraway, salt and pepper. Simmer until liquid has reduced by two-thirds. Remove from the heat; stir in mashed potatoes. Refrigerate until chilled.

For mustard sauce, combine the cream and mustard in a small saucepan. Bring to a boil. Reduce heat; simmer until sauce is reduced to preferred thickness.

Form the potato mixture into four to six balls; flatten into thick patties and dust with flour. Fry in ¼ inch of oil over medium heat until a golden crust forms on both sides. Drizzle mustard sauce over patties or serve as a dipping sauce.

Serves 2-3

# Zwiebelkuchen

*Karen and Fred Grampp were two of our first VIPs and share a common German heritage. We met Fred and Karen for the first time on the day of our son Paul's Hatting Ceremony. As is tradition, at age 16, Paul began his official apprenticeship with his father to learn about wine and vine.*

*Karen shared this recipe from Marianne Grampp, Fred's cousin in Lohmar, Germany, where it was served at Winefests along the Mosel River.*

### Dough

1 cake compressed yeast *or* 1 package (¹/₄ ounce) active
 dry yeast
¹/₂ cup lukewarm milk
2¹/₂ cups all-purpose flour
2 eggs
7 tablespoons butter
Pinch salt

### Filling

4¹/₂ pounds onions, quartered and thinly sliced
¹/₂ cup butter
¹/₄ cup diced bacon
4 eggs
Pinch salt
1 cup (8 ounces) sour cream
3 tablespoons all-purpose flour
Pinch caraway seed

In a mixing bowl, soften yeast in milk. Add the remaining dough ingredients; knead until smooth. Cover and let rise in a warm place for 30 minutes. Meanwhile, in a large skillet, sauté onions in butter until translucent. Remove and set aside. In the same skillet, sauté bacon lightly. In a large bowl, combine the bacon, eggs, salt, sour cream, flour and caraway seed. Add onions.

On a lightly floured board, roll out dough. Place in a jelly roll pan. Pour filling over dough. Bake at 425° for 1 hour.

Serves 8

# Putting Down Roots in the Country

Looking for our Ponderosa, we purchased from one of Paul's physical therapy patients 100 acres on a gravel road called Poor Farm Road. At the highest elevation in Brazos County, it had a nice lake and constant breezes, which ultimately provided a nice microclimate for growing grapes. The mobile home on the property became our home.

Country solitude was perfect. There were few neighbors for miles, and they all farmed. Fortunately, we had a next-door neighbor who saved us on many occasions during our evolution to farmers. He must have laughed every night with tales of these new "citified" neighbors.

He taught us how to drive a tractor on steep inclines without being thrown to the ground, and

he came to the rescue our first winter, when our water pipes froze solid. He told me to gather some snow in a saucepan and melt it on my gas stove. At his instruction, I brought the melted snow to a boil and took the pan outside, where I poured the boiling water on the pipes under the mobile home. For more than an hour, I repeated the process over and over to no avail.

When I called and told him his plan was not working, he came over. Patiently watching me complete the process one more time, he observed, with a grin on his face, that I was pouring the boiling water on the copper gas line rather than the frozen water line. Within no time, water was flowing. He was such a provision for us. —Merrill

23

# Treberwurst (Wine-Soaked Bratwurst)

*The German harvest tradition of serving Treberwurst became an annual harvest tradition at Messina Hof as well. In Germany and Switzerland, the harvesters would bring sausage and bratwurst, which they would pack in the skins and seeds (what we call "must") of the grapes. The meat would marinate and bake over coals. After the picking, the harvesters would eat the Treberwurst with crusty breads and mustards.*

5 pounds Lenoir grape seeds and skins
1 gallon water
4 cups red wine vinegar
1/2 bottle Messina Hof Merlot
1/2 bottle Messina Hof Pinot Noir
1/2 bottle Messina Hof Cabernet Sauvignon
5 pounds bratwurst *or* your favorite sausages

In a large crock, combine the grape seeds and skins, water, vinegar and wines. Add bratwurst; soak for at least 2 days. Remove sausages from brine, then grill or roast.

Serves 15

# Planting the Roots of the Vineyard

Physical therapy brought Paul to Bryan. Through physical therapy, a patient planted the idea for us to plant a vineyard. Ron Perry, a graduate student at Texas A&M, was led to Paul's private practice, the Sports and Back Clinic, to find healing from a sports injury. During his sessions, Ron talked about his thesis on grape growing in Texas. When he learned of Paul's family background and our recently acquired acreage, Ron suggested that Paul and I plant an experimental vineyard for research. With enthusiasm, we accepted the challenge.

Paul was very busy with two full-time jobs—along with his clinic, he was director of physical therapy for St. Joseph Hospital—so my days were spent laying irrigation pipe and planting vines in our 1-acre experimental vineyard.

Each vine looked like a stick protruding from the ground identified only with a handwritten sign. Day after day, kindly farmers would drive by and stop to ask me what I was doing. Inevitably they'd say something like, "Honey, don't you know that grapes don't grow in Texas?" Or "Those things look like dead sticks … are you sure they're alive?"

There were only three wineries in the state when we started Messina Hof. No one believed that grapes would live, nor did they believe that good wine could be made from grapes sourced in Texas. In fact, the *Chicago Tribune* ran a cartoon of two cowboys sitting at the campfire; one asked the other if he would prefer Blush or Chardonnay. "Chateau Bubba" became the joke of the time.

As Paul and I researched grape growing, we found that our property had perfect soil PH and perfect elevation for breezes that kept the humidity low on the leaves. Plus, the two lakes on the property provided cooling tanks.

Once the vineyard was planted, we began the process of producing experimental batches of wine. Our 1981 Lenoir/Cabernet Sauvignon blend won gold at the State Fair of Texas competition.

You can tell when something is meant to be. It's not something you can take credit for doing. It's something you were born to fulfill. Paul was born to be a winemaker and a vine-tender. As a physical therapist, he had honed his skills as a people-tender. Vine-tending was just a natural progression.

In 1982, we planted our second vineyard (which we planted in the snow), began converting the mobile home into a winery and harvested a son. Paul Mitchell Bonarrigo was born in April that year. —*Merrill*

# Angel's Peach Cobbler

*To pay tribute to my German heritage, Paul created Angel Late Harvest Riesling. Angel was made from grapes harvested at the end of the growing season when almost raisined. Its flavor, reminiscent of angelic nectar, inspired the name. The first vintage received a 90 score in the Wine Spectator.*

8 cups sliced peaches
2 cups packed brown sugar
6 tablespoons butter
2 tablespoons lemon juice
1 cup Messina Hof Angel Riesling
4 teaspoons cornstarch
1/2 cup cold water
*Topping*
2 cups all-purpose flour
1 cup sugar
2 teaspoons baking powder
Pinch salt
1 cup butter, softened
1/2 cup cold water

In a large saucepan, combine the peaches, brown sugar, butter and lemon juice. Cook until fruit is soft. Add wine. Dissolve cornstarch in cold water; add enough of the mixture to the peaches to thicken. Pour into a greased 3-quart baking dish or individual baking dishes.

For topping, in a bowl, combine flour, sugar, baking powder and salt. Mix in softened butter. Slowly add water until mixture is a loose batter. Spoon over fruit. Bake at 350° until cobbler is set and topping is golden brown. Serve warm with a scoop of homemade vanilla ice cream.

Serves 10-12

# Harvest Becomes a Family Affair

The first harvest, in 1983, was anticipated like the birth of a child. Each day Paul checked the brix (sugar content) of the grapes with a refractometer. When the sugar was right, we scheduled a pick for the next morning. Rising with the sun, the family proceeded to the vineyard, only to find that mockingbirds had consumed all of the grapes.

After working with Texas A&M on this situation, we added computerized hawk horns that gave off attack screeches over the vineyard. They were so effective that two real hawks moved into the area looking for the source of the sounds.

We began sharing the harvest experience by showing a video during tours of the winery. A tour in those days entailed tasting in our home and a walk through the mobile home winery.

Merrill and Paul VI

In 1984, 14 international Texas A&M students called to ask if they could help us pick our Bryan vineyard. It was a tradition in their European village that all the residents gathered and picked the grapes, broke bread together and shared good times. The next year, those 14 students brought an additional 14 friends, and the Messina Hof family expanded.

Year after year, the picking crews grew. The harvest at Messina Hof is truly a family affair, where each participant sees the entire cycle of winemaking from the grape to the glass. By 1993, harvesting at the estate vineyard was by reservation only.

Merrill's sister, Monie Smith

At the conclusion of each picking day, wines from the previous vintage are served with foods created with the wines and with regional ingredients. As the vineyard grew, we added vegetable and herb gardens on the estate. We now have a red wine herb garden and a white wine herb garden featuring herbs that have natural affinities to those styles of wines. (For more about herb and wine pairings, see pages 100–101.) —*Merrill*

Paul V

# *Port Honors the "Pauls"*

Papa Paulo Texas Port rolled out in the winter of 1984. As a tribute to Paul and the "Pauls" who had been the winemakers for previous generations and to the style of wine they made in Sicily, Papa Paulo spoke to the Italian heritage of Messina Hof.

We used an unknown grape called Lenoir, also known as Black Spanish. It means "The black." While the origin is unknown, it is a red grape that flows free-run black juice. The cluster is beautiful and can achieve 1½ pounds. Lenoir instantly fell in love with the Brazos Valley.

The challenge was to take this little-known grape and make a world-class product out of our estate vineyard. Our first port was made in the traditional way of the Portuguese. We harvested the 1983 Lenoir at 26% sugar and fermented it until 8% sugar, then we added high-proof brandy. This brought the alcohol content to 18%. It was then aged in new American oak until the wine was bottled.

Papa Paulo Port was an instant success. It was a dessert by itself, went perfectly with everything chocolate, and paired surprisingly well with gingerbread and Stilton cheese. (To try some port pairings, see Papa Paulo Texas Port and Pecan Tasties on page 143, Chocolate Pâté on page 144 and Gingerbread on page 145.) —*Merrill*

# An Introduction to Italian-American Cooking

Prior to our first trip to New York so Merrill could meet the family, I taught her in Italian to say, "Yesterday it was hot." I didn't tell her what it meant. I said, "Don't worry about it; just say it and Nonna will love it." Unfortunately, the day she met Nonna, it was 32 degrees and snowing. I guess the next time I will have to teach her more Italian. —*Paul*

When Paul took me back to Little Italy to meet Nona Bonarrigo, grandmother and matriarch of the Bonarrigo family and her clan, I learned what *real* Italian-American cooking was all about. After Paul and I made a trip to Arturo's bakery and the Arthur Avenue market, Nona allowed me to assist her in the kitchen.

We made antipasto, dandelion salad, pasta with spaghetti sauce, veal cutlets and dressed raw clams. What a feast! I thought the whole neighborhood must be coming for dinner. There were 40 veal cutlets alone! To my surprise, there were only five for dinner.

The food was piled high, and a gallon jug of red wine from the family barrels in the basement was set on the table. Everything was delicious ... and just when I thought we were finished, she brought in miniature pastries from Arturo's and port for dessert. —*Merrill*

Paul's dad did burlesque comedy in New York. As a child, Paul loved to work with his dad on routines and entertain with him. It's easy to see how he turned into such a performer.

# Marinara Sauce

*The Bonarrigo family was very protective of their special wine recipe. It was never shared with any other family. Tastings of the different barrels during aging stimulated conversation of whose recipe was best, whose oak was best, whose palate was best, and on and on. The pride of the Italian family was in the wine and the sauce.*

*This recipe makes a large amount, but it freezes well, so when we don't have a large group, we save some for later use.*

4 onions, diced
5 tablespoons minced garlic
2 tablespoons olive oil
2 bottles Messina Hof Papa Paulo Port

3 cups diced tomatoes
3 cups tomato sauce
1 1/2 cups tomato paste
1/2 pound fresh basil, minced
1 tablespoon cracked red pepper
1/2 cup sugar

In a large saucepan, sauté onions and garlic in oil until translucent. Add wine and cook until onions are caramelized. Add remaining ingredients; cook until sauce reaches desired thickness, stirring occasionally. Taste and add more sugar if desired.

Makes about 3 quarts

# Salmoriglio (Sicilian Sauce)

1 cup olive oil
1/4 cup hot water
Juice of 2 lemons
1/4 cup finely chopped parsley
2 1/2 teaspoons minced fresh oregano
Salt to taste

In a warm bowl, whisk the oil, gradually adding water, lemon juice, parsley and oregano. Season with salt. Warm the sauce in a double boiler until hot. Pour over roasted meat or baked fish and serve immediately.

Makes about 1½ cups

# Sicilian Meatball Soup

*Winter months are great for soups. When Paul worked late, soup would keep until he got home. This is one of our favorites.*

¹/₂ pound ground lean beef
1 egg
2 tablespoons Italian breadcrumbs
8 teaspoons grated Parmesan cheese
2 to 3 sprigs parsley
1 clove garlic, minced
Salt and pepper to taste
7¹/₂ cups beef stock
1 cup fresh spinach
¹/₂ pound tagliatelle ribbon noodles
Minced fresh basil and additional grated Parmesan
   cheese

In a bowl, combine the beef, egg, breadcrumbs, Parmesan cheese, parsley, garlic, salt and pepper; knead until smooth. Roll into balls about 1 inch in diameter.

In a saucepan or soup pot, bring stock to a boil. Add meatballs and spinach; simmer for 5 minutes. Add the noodles; cook until tender but still firm. Serve immediately; sprinkle basil and Parmesan on top.

*Serves 6*

The Bronx was an incubator for musical talent in the 1960s. Paul grew up listening to Dion and the Belmonts singing on his street corner. He put himself through college in a band called the Brookwoods that he formed with a group of great friends (shown left to right: Paul, Frank Lawrence, Sal Rizzo, Dan Depolito and Dave Carter). Another member, Jim Richard (not pictured), played sax. Paul played bass and was the lead singer.  They played at a club with the Loving Spoonfuls and were the opening act for Guy Lombardo at the 1964 New York World's Fair.

# Paulo's Salad

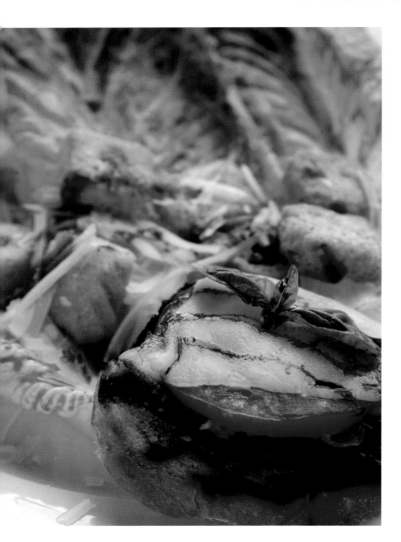

*When Paul's grandfather came to America from Sicily, he brought his recipe for a salad that became famous as a wedding proposal salad.*

3 anchovies
1 tablespoon minced garlic
2 tablespoons Messina Hof Port
2 tablespoons soy sauce
2 tablespoons Dijon mustard
2 tablespoons olive oil
2 tablespoons balsamic vinegar
2 tablespoons lemon juice
1 egg
12 whole romaine leaves
¼ cup croutons
2 tablespoons grated Romano cheese
Basil Prosciutto Crostini (recipe on page 90)

At tableside, combine the anchovies, garlic, wine, soy sauce, mustard, oil, vinegar, lemon juice and egg in a bowl; mix well. Rinse romaine in water and shake off excess. Submerge each leaf in the dressing, shaking off excess until the dressing appears as droplets. Fan romaine on salad plates; top with croutons and Romano cheese. Serve with crostini. Salad is intended to be eaten with fingers instead of a fork.

Serves 2

# The Legend of Paulo's Salad

The year is 1860 in Messina, Sicily, a small village on the northeast coast of Sicily. Paulo Bonarrigo III, a prominent family winemaker, has fallen madly in love with Antoinette Borghia, the most beautiful woman in all of Sicily. As was the custom, Paulo wanted to ask Antoinette's father for her hand in marriage. So, he invited Antoinette and all of her family over for dinner on a Saturday evening. His purpose at dinner was to ask Antoinette's father for her hand.

Since Paulo was the family winemaker and this Saturday was the beginning of a bountiful harvest, he was extremely busy. To make matters worse, some of the vineyard workers didn't come to work, so Paulo had more to do than expected.

Late that Saturday afternoon, Paulo realized he hadn't gathered any of the food for his very important dinner that evening. In fact, Antoinette's family would arrive at Paulo's house in less than a half hour. He had little choice. He dashed into his garden to see what he could find that was unique, creative ... and took less than 30 minutes to prepare.

This is when he created Paulo's Salad. He chose anchovies to represent the depth of his love for Antoinette, since anchovies symbolically represent the great depths of the sea. He chose romaine lettuce to represent the freshness of Antoinette's beauty ... like the freshness of his garden. Naturally,

Paulo III

he chose his family wine to use in the salad dressing.

Antoinette and her family came for dinner, and Paulo prepared the food before their very eyes. Antoinette's father was so impressed that when Paulo asked for his daughter's hand, he gladly blessed their marriage.

# Paulo Roasted Potato Salad

*Paul immersed me in the Italian tradition and food. No wonder they are such a robust and proud people ... their lives revolve around family and celebration. In no time, Sicilian recipes became staples in our home.*

2 1/2 pounds baby new potatoes
1 medium onion, sliced
1/4 cup olive oil, *divided*
2 tablespoons snipped fresh rosemary
1 clove garlic, minced
1/2 teaspoon *each* salt and black pepper
2 tablespoons balsamic vinegar
2 tablespoons Messina Hof Paulo Meritage
2 tablespoons Messina Hof Sauvignon Blanc Jalapeño
   Mustard *or* spicy brown mustard of your choice
1 medium red bell pepper, julienned
3 tablespoons pine nuts, toasted

Toss the potatoes and onion with 2 tablespoons oil, rosemary, garlic, salt and pepper. Place in a single layer in a well-greased shallow baking pan. Bake at 450° for 25–30 minutes or until potatoes are tender and golden brown, stirring twice. Transfer to a large bowl; set aside.

In a small bowl, whisk the vinegar, wine, mustard and remaining oil. Pour over potato mixture; add red pepper and toss gently. Top with pine nuts.

Serves 8

# Tonno alla Messinese
# (Tuna from the Straits of Messina)

2 onions, sliced
2 ribs celery, diced
1 clove garlic, minced
1¼ cups olive oil
1 pound ripe tomatoes, peeled, seeded and chopped
½ cup Messina Hof Pinot Grigio
1 pound potatoes, peeled and cubed
8 to 10 large pitted green olives
4 tablespoons golden seedless raisins
2½ tablespoons capers
2½ tablespoons pine nuts
2 teaspoons minced fresh basil
1 teaspoon minced fresh oregano
Salt to taste
6 tuna steaks

In a large skillet, sauté the onions, celery and garlic in oil. As soon as the onions are translucent, add tomatoes and wine. Bring to a gentle boil. Add the potatoes, olives, raisins, capers, pine nuts, basil and oregano. Simmer for 30 minutes, stirring occasionally. Add a little water if sauce is too thick. Season with salt. Grill the tuna steaks; serve hot with sauce.

*Serves 6*

# Braciole di Pescespada
# (Stuffed Swordfish Sicilian Style)

*Our first vintner dinner was in San Angelo, Texas. Eight people attended. One man came because he thought a vintner was a Christian church social. When the wine steward presented him the cork for the first wine, he had no idea what to do with it. The man looked at the cork, tossed it in the air and looked for approval. Receiving none and out of sheer frustration, he took the cork to his mouth and ate it. The table was shocked into instant silence.*

*The wine steward was mature beyond his years. Looking at the man with great sincerity, he said, "I am so glad you did that. More and more people are chewing the cork to check it these days."*

*At that dinner, we served Braciole di Pescespada and Pomodori alla Siciliana.*

½ pound plus 6 thin slices of swordfish
1 small onion, finely chopped
1¼ cups olive oil
2½ tablespoons brandy
Salt to taste
2½ tablespoons soft breadcrumbs
6 slices mozzarella cheese
2 to 3 sprigs basil, finely chopped
Pinch minced thyme
Freshly ground black pepper
Salmoriglio Sauce (recipe on page 31)
1 to 2 lemons, sliced

Cut the ½ pound of swordfish into small pieces; set the thinly sliced fish aside. Heat oil in a saucepan or skillet; sauté the small pieces of fish and onion. As soon as the onion begins to brown, add brandy and sprinkle with salt. When the brandy has evaporated, remove from the heat. Stir in breadcrumbs.

Spread the mixture over each thin slice of swordfish. Cover with a slice of mozzarella; sprinkle with basil, thyme and pepper. Roll up the slices to enclose the filling and tie with kitchen string. Broil or grill the swordfish rolls, over charcoal if possible, for 15 minutes or less (the heat should not be too fierce). Serve immediately with Salmoriglio Sauce and lemon slices.

Serves 6

# Pomodori alla Siciliana
# (Baked Stuffed Tomatoes)

8 large ripe tomatoes
1 onion, finely chopped
Olive oil
8 anchovy fillets, pounded to paste
1 bunch fresh parsley, chopped
3 tablespoons capers
2 tablespoons breadcrumbs
¼ cup sliced ripe olives
Salt, pepper and ground nutmeg to taste

Cut a thin slice off the top of each tomato and set aside. Scoop out some of the pulp; seed, chop and set aside. Invert tomatoes onto paper towels to drain. In a skillet, sauté onion in a small amount of oil. Add chopped tomato pulp, anchovy paste, parsley, capers, breadcrumbs and olives. Season with salt, pepper and a little nutmeg; mix well. Stuff into tomato shells; replace tops. Place in a baking dish; drizzle with olive oil. Bake, uncovered, at 350° for 30 minutes.

Serves 8

# Almond Anise Biscotti

*Paul's mom, Rose Bonarrigo, made biscotti, which we enjoyed with Italian espresso and anisette.*

$1/4$ cup butter, softened
$1/2$ cup sugar
$1/2$ cup packed brown sugar
2 teaspoons anise seed
3 eggs
$1/4$ teaspoon almond extract
3 cups sifted all-purpose flour
3 teaspoons baking powder
$1/2$ cup chopped almonds

In a mixing bowl, beat butter and sugars until well blended. Beat in anise seed, eggs and extract. Combine flour and baking powder; add to sugar mixture and mix well. Stir in almonds. (Dough should be firm; add extra flour if it's too sticky.)

Shape dough into two 10-inch x 1-inch rolls. Place 4 inches apart on a greased baking sheet. Flatten each roll to 2-inch width. Bake at 350° for 20–30 minutes or until golden brown. Cool completely. Cut diagonally into ½-inch slices. Place cut side down on ungreased baking sheets. Bake for 6–10 minutes or until bottoms begin to brown; turn and bake 3–5 minutes longer or until crisp. Cool completely.

Makes 3 dozen

# Recipes From the Villa

## A HOME FOR THE EXTENDED MESSINA HOF FAMILY

*"Do not forget to entertain strangers, for by so doing some people have entertained angels without knowing it."*
*Hebrews 13:2 (NIV)*

Every guest at Messina Hof was considered a member of our extended family. We wanted to create a home away from home for all of our guests and to provide that unique Texas Wine Country getaway food-and-wine experience.

Wine is an old-world beverage with a long history. Messina Hof represented that heritage and needed an appropriate home. At the turn of the 20th century, the Ursuline Sisters of Galveston moved to Bryan after the great storm destroyed their school. They built a beautiful place to train girls, many of whom were sisters of Aggies.

In the 1930s, the property was purchased by William Howell, who was appointed U.S. Ambassador to Uruguay by President Truman, and he turned the building into his family's manor home. Later, it became part of Allen Academy. Messina Hof purchased the property in 1982, dismantled the building brick by brick and moved it to the vineyard site.

The Villa at Messina Hof took root in 1997 through a competition of the senior architecture students at Texas A&M. Each student submitted a design to fulfill our wine country getaway vision, utilizing the materials from the Ursuline Academy building. Two students were chosen to collaborate on the final design, incorporating architectural pieces collected over 15 years. Monie Smith of Serious Moonlighting (my sister) and I did the interior design and decoration of the Villa, which opened October 28, 1999.

We filled the inn with family heirlooms and unique antiques, such as Louis Pasteur's country French doors ... hand-rubbed bronze stair railings ... 100-year-old stained-glass windows ... and furnishings from as early as 1600. Each of the 10 guest rooms tells a different story from a memorable moment in history. Some are romantic, like the Napoleon & Josephine room, which is furnished in a luxurious French manner. The Thomas Jefferson room, on the other hand, has a masculine décor honoring the "grandfather of American wines."

Couples love to stroll through the vineyard, watch turtles by the lake, or sit in the rocking chairs on the patio and sip wine as they look out over the vineyard. Each season features different themed floral arrangements, table décor and breakfast menus.

Guests dine together at a gourmet champagne breakfast each morning in the Great Room. In the evening, they enjoy Messina Hof wines and specialty cheeses ... and they find famous Messina Hof Port wine chocolate truffles on their pillows. In 2005, the Villa was voted the most romantic inn in the United States. —*Merrill*

# Eggs Florentine

2 tablespoons butter
1 cup fresh spinach
3 cups heavy whipping cream
¼ cup Messina Hof Pinot Grigio
2 teaspoons granulated garlic
Salt and pepper to taste
4 slices Canadian bacon, warmed
2 English muffins, split and toasted
4 eggs, poached
4 tablespoons shredded cheddar cheese

In a saucepan, heat butter; add spinach and cook until it begins to wilt. Add cream, wine and garlic; reduce until sauce thickens. Season with salt and pepper. Place a slice of Canadian bacon on each English muffin half; top with a poached egg, spinach cream sauce and cheddar cheese. Serve with breakfast potatoes.

*Serves 2*

# Strata Milano

1 loaf (1 pound) sourdough bread
5 eggs
3¼ cups milk
1 cup ricotta cheese
½ cup crumbled feta cheese
1 teaspoon salt
½ teaspoon cayenne pepper
1¾ cups diced tomatoes
1 cup chopped red onion
6 slices bacon, cooked and crumbled
1½ teaspoons dried rosemary, crushed
Freshly grated Parmesan cheese
Paprika

Cut bread into 1-inch slices; toast and cut into cubes. In a mixing bowl, whisk the eggs, milk, cheeses, salt and cayenne until well blended. Combine the tomatoes, onion, bacon and rosemary. Place half of the bread cubes in a greased 13-inch x 9-inch x 2-inch baking dish; top with half of the tomato mixture and egg mixture. Repeat layers. Sprinkle with Parmesan and paprika. Cover and refrigerate for 8 hours or overnight.

Remove from the refrigerator 30 minutes before baking. Bake, uncovered, at 350° for 45–60 minutes or until a knife comes out clean. Let stand for 15 minutes before serving.

*Serves 6-8*

# Messina Hof Poached Eggs

*This is one of our signature breakfast dishes featuring a crab and potato hash topped with poached eggs and shrimp.*

5 tablespoons olive oil, *divided*
1 cooked potato, diced
4 tablespoons diced shallots
2 tablespoons minced garlic
4 tablespoons crabmeat
3 eggs, poached
3 shrimp, peeled and deveined
$\frac{1}{2}$ cup Messina Hof Chenin Blanc
Juice of 1 lemon
2 tablespoons butter
2 tablespoons chopped fresh basil
Salt and pepper to taste

In a sauté pan, heat 4 tablespoons oil. Add potatoes, shallots and garlic; once potatoes begin to brown, stir in the crab. Transfer to a serving dish. Top with poached eggs; keep warm. In the same pan, heat remaining oil. Add shrimp; cook until shrimp begin to turn pink. Add wine, lemon juice and butter; cook until reduced. Spoon shrimp and sauce over eggs; sprinkle with basil, salt and pepper.

Serves 1-3

# Villa Fiesta Brunch

6 corn tortillas, cut into $\frac{1}{2}$-inch strips

1 pound bulk pork *or* turkey sausage, cooked and drained

16 slices pepper Jack cheese

1 can (4 ounces) chopped green chilies

8 eggs

$\frac{1}{2}$ cup milk

3 tablespoons Messina Hof Garlic Merlot Dressing *or* ranch salad dressing

$\frac{1}{2}$ teaspoon garlic salt

$\frac{1}{2}$ teaspoon chili powder

2 large tomatoes, thinly sliced

Paprika

Salsa and sour cream

In a greased 13-inch x 9-inch x 2-inch baking dish, arrange half of the tortilla strips, sausage and cheese slices. Layer with remaining tortilla strips and sausage; sprinkle with chilies. Top with remaining cheese. In a large bowl, whisk the eggs, milk, dressing, garlic salt and chili powder. Pour over cheese. Arrange tomato slices over the top; sprinkle with paprika. Cover and refrigerate overnight.

Remove from the refrigerator 30 minutes before baking. Bake, uncovered, at 350° for 20–25 minutes or until center is set and edges are lightly browned. Cut into squares; serve with salsa and sour cream.

*Serves 10*

## Chenin Blanc Strikes Gold

In 1983, we planted the third vineyard, officially opened Messina Hof winery and fought the mockingbirds for our first commercial crop.

The winery at that time was an enclosed carport, and the living room was converted into a tasting room. The kitchen became the lab. When we found out a dairy in Anderson, Texas, was closing, Paul and I hooked up a trailer and hauled their milk tanks to our property to use for wine.

We finally released our first wine in October of 1983—our estate Chenin Blanc. Eight producing acres of grapes produced 1,300 gallons of wine in that first year. Each bottle was christened with a birth certificate and number. The vintage sold out in 3 months, and it won gold medals in every competition we entered.

Each year, the Brazos Valley Chenin Blanc got better. In 1986, the *Wine Spectator* described it as having an aroma of rose petals and gave it the highest score given to date for a Texas wine.

Our next release was Texas Cabernet Sauvignon 1983. It, too, was a success. We were on a roll. —*Merrill*

# Blintz French Toast

12 slices cinnamon-raisin bread, crusts removed
*Cheesecake Filling*
1 package (8 ounces) cream cheese, softened
$1/4$ cup milk
1 egg, lightly beaten
3 tablespoons sugar
1 tablespoon lemon zest
*Custard*
3 eggs
1 cup milk
1 cup (8 ounces) sour cream
$1/4$ cup sugar
$1/2$ teaspoon vanilla extract
Confectioners' sugar
Fresh berries *or* sliced peaches

Place six slices of bread in a greased 13-inch x 9-inch x 2-inch baking dish. In a mixing bowl, beat the filling ingredients. Spread evenly over bread. Top with remaining bread. For custard, beat the eggs, milk, sour cream, sugar and vanilla; pour evenly over all. Refrigerate for 1 hour or until bread is evenly moistened.

Loosely tent with foil. Bake at 350° for 50–60 minutes or until top is golden brown.

Cut into six servings. Dust with confectioners' sugar and top with fruit.

Serves 6

# French Toast
# with Strawberry-Rhubarb Sauce

2 cups sliced fresh strawberries
1 cup chopped fresh rhubarb
2 ½ cups Messina Hof Ivory Ports of Call
1 ½ cups water
½ cup sugar
½ cup packed brown sugar
3 eggs
¾ cup milk
Zest of 1 orange
½ teaspoon vanilla extract
8 slices French bread (1 inch thick)
Butter

In a saucepan, combine the strawberries, rhubarb, wine, water and sugars. Bring to a boil; reduce heat. Simmer, uncovered, until rhubarb is soft and begins to fall apart.

In a shallow bowl, whisk the eggs, milk, orange zest and vanilla. Dip French bread into batter; cook on a hot griddle in butter until golden brown on both sides.

Strain sauce and adjust sweetness; serve with French toast.

Serves 4

*"The art of entertaining is truly an attitude of the heart. At Messina Hof, each guest is an extended member of our family. We delight in memories made here and passions shared while picking grapes in the vineyard or over a glass of wine." —Merrill*

*These are our most popular sauces to serve over crêpes, pancakes and French toast.*

# Pinot Grigio Applesauce

1 cup chopped apples
3 tablespoons butter
½ cup packed brown sugar
¼ cup Messina Hof Pinot Grigio

In a saucepan, sauté apples in butter until tender. Add brown sugar; cook until the sugar begins to caramelize the apples. Add wine; reduce until liquid reaches the consistency of syrup.

Makes about ½ cup

# Strawberry Port Wine Sauce

¾ cup water
1½ cups sugar
1½ cups fresh strawberries, chopped
1 cup strawberry *or* raspberry jelly
½ cup Messina Hof Tawny Port

In a saucepan, bring water to a boil. Add sugar and stir until dissolved. Add strawberries; reduce until liquid reaches the consistency of syrup. Add jelly and wine; heat through. Cook until sauce reaches desired consistency.

Makes about 2 cups

# Spinach Bacon Quiche

*On Sunday mornings, Paul and I would pamper each other by serving a unique breakfast in bed. One Sunday when it was his turn, Paul walked across the living room from the bedroom to the kitchen, still in his underwear. Out of the corner of his eye, he saw a family sitting on the sofa!*

*Paul kept moving nonchalantly to the kitchen, where he put on an apron and invited the family to stay for breakfast. As it turned out, they had heard about our winery tours, and when they arrived, they found the front door unlocked. They had the most personal tour of all time. Years later, Paul met this same family at a festival, where they shared memories of that revealing day.*

3 slices peppered smoked bacon, diced
1½ cups chopped fresh spinach
½ cup diced onion
6 eggs
1½ cups heavy whipping cream
1 cup (4 ounces) shredded mozzarella cheese
1 pastry shell (9 inches), prebaked

In a skillet, sauté the bacon, spinach and onion. In a mixing bowl, beat the eggs; whisk in the cream. Stir in the mozzarella. Spoon bacon mixture into pastry shell. Add egg mixture, stirring with a fork to distribute ingredients evenly. Bake at 350° for 40–45 minutes.

Serves 6

# Fermenting on the Move

By 1985, other farmers were growing grapes around Texas. Grape growing and winemaking is like a marriage. Great wine can only be made from great grapes ... grape growers and winemakers must be of like mind. The 1985 harvest was going to be exciting.

I decided to harvest the grapes in Halfway, Texas, and process the fruit in the carport of one of my growers, Pete Laney, a prominent Texas legislator. At sunrise, we started processing Zinfandel from the vineyard of Freddie and Rodney Bell, great friends to this day. It took all day, weighing one harvest bucket at a time. Grandmother Bell recorded the weight of each bucket. Juice spilled all over the driveway.

Finally, after 20 hours, and my white shirt and shorts a purple mess, the pressing was over. The result was 1,400 gallons of White Zin successfully tucked away in a 2,000-gallon tank strapped to a rental flatbed truck.

Twelve hours later, after driving through many dry Texas counties and fermenting as we went, I pulled into the winery. Merrill looked relieved and so was I. She offloaded the White Zinfandel and did the lab. Wow, it was fermented to exactly where we wanted it. Later, we laughed about this moving fermenter making wine as it traveled through one dry county after another! This was the first moving winery in Texas.

While I slept, Merrill chilled the wine down to 30°F and fined it. The next week, we filtered the

wine, bottled it and submitted it in an International Wine competition on the East Coast. Lo and behold, it won Best of Class and the Gold Medal. So our first International gold was made with a most unusual process and technique.

The competition invited me to New York to share the secrets of our success with this wine. When I told them how it was made, I got the sense they didn't believe me. They must have thought it was a Texas tall tale.

It didn't help matters when I was asked about the location of Halfway, Texas. I explained it was 10 miles west of Quarterway, which was 10 miles west of the Jimmy Dean Sausage factory in Plainview. When I asked them what town they thought came

10 miles after Halfway, they guessed correctly—Three Quarterway. Then I asked what they thought came after Three Quarterway, and they guessed All the Way. What do you think? Actually, there is absolutely nothing 10 miles past Three Quarterway. I just tell everybody that it means people up there can't go all the way!

That was the first and last time we ever processed fruit in the vineyard. Since then, we have picked the grapes and transported them in refrigerated trucks to the winery. The fruit is picked at 70°F and transported at 32°. The grapes crisp up, and the skins of the grapes soak in the cool juice.

Each year, the red grapes of Cabernet Sauvignon and Merlot would create dark juice that would become darker as the juice soaked in the skins. When California later started talking about "cold soaking" skins for improved color of red wines, little did they know we had discovered the effect 10 years earlier out of the transportation necessities across Texas during the heat of summer. —*Paul*

# Puffy Pancake

*Mama Rosa Bonarrigo always made her pancakes like this and then cut them into wedges or squares to serve. The batter may be made a day ahead and chilled overnight.*

2 eggs, lightly beaten
¹/₂ cup all-purpose flour
¹/₂ cup milk
Pinch salt
Pinch freshly grated nutmeg
3 tablespoons unsalted butter
Confectioners' sugar

In a mixing bowl, whisk eggs, flour milk, salt and nutmeg until well combined (batter may be slightly lumpy). In an ovenproof skillet, melt butter. When skillet is hot, add the batter. Immediately place in a preheated 425° oven. Bake for 10 minutes or until puffed and golden brown. Dust with confectioners' sugar and serve immediately.

Serves 2

# Date Nut Bread with Port

4 eggs, *separated*
1 cup raw sugar
¹/₄ cup butter
1 cup all-purpose flour
2 teaspoons baking powder
¹/₂ teaspoon salt
¹/₄ teaspoon ground allspice
2 teaspoons vanilla extract
2 pounds chopped dates
4 cups chopped pecans
¹/₃ cup Messina Hof Papa Paulo Texas Port

In a large mixing bowl, beat egg yolks. Add the sugar, butter, flour, baking powder, salt, allspice and vanilla; mix thoroughly with hands or a spoon. In a small mixing bowl, beat egg whites until soft peaks form; fold into batter. Fold in dates. Toss pecans with port; fold into batter.

Pour into a greased tube pan or two loaf pans. Bake at 300° for 50 minutes or until a toothpick inserted near the center comes out clean.

Makes 1-2 loaves

# Banana Bread with Muscat

1 cup sugar
1/2 cup butter, softened
2 eggs
1 cup mashed bananas
1 tablespoon Messina Hof Muscat Canelli
2 cups all-purpose flour
1 teaspoon salt
1 teaspoon baking powder
1/2 teaspoon baking soda
1/2 cup chopped pecans

In a mixing bowl, beat the sugar, butter, eggs, bananas and wine until blended. Combine the flour, salt, baking powder and baking soda; beat into banana mixture. Stir in pecans. Pour into a greased loaf pan. Let stand for 20 minutes. Bake at 350° for 1 hour.

Makes 1 loaf

# Southern Butter Biscuits

2 cups unsifted all-purpose flour
1 tablespoon double-acting baking powder
1/2 teaspoon salt
1/4 teaspoon baking soda
1/3 cup cold butter
3/4 cup buttermilk
Melted butter
Pure maple syrup *or* honey

In a large bowl, combine flour, baking powder, salt and baking soda. With a pastry blender, cut in butter until mixture resembles coarse crumbs. Add buttermilk; stir only until crumbs stick together. Refrigerate until firm. Turn dough onto a lightly floured pastry board; knead 8–10 times to mix thoroughly. Refrigerate until chilled.

On a lightly floured pastry board, roll out dough to ½-inch thickness. With a floured biscuit cutter, cut into 2-inch rounds. Place 1 inch apart on an ungreased baking sheet. Brush lightly with melted butter; stack another biscuit on top of each biscuit. Bake at 425° for 15–20 minutes or until light golden brown. Serve immediately with syrup or honey.

## Makes 6 large biscuits

*"Every weekend our home was filled with guests experiencing our Texas wines. I offered experiments of wine and food for each tour and recorded the guests' responses. I wasn't really sure if the tours were increasing because of the wine or because of the free entertainment and food." —Merrill*

# No-Knead Company Rolls

*In order to train our palates on the effects of herbs and spices on wine, I rolled cream cheese balls in different herbs and spices. Each seasoned ball was tasted with different wines and homemade bread or rolls.*

1 cake compressed yeast

1 cup lukewarm milk

2 eggs, beaten

¹/₂ cup sugar

³/₄ teaspoon salt

4¹/₂ cups whole-wheat flour, *divided*

¹/₄ cup butter, melted

In a mixing bowl, dissolve yeast in warm milk. Add the eggs, sugar and salt; mix well. Add 2¼ cups flour; mix well. Add butter and remaining flour. Cover and let rise in a warm draft-free place until doubled. Roll into 2-inch balls. Place on a greased baking sheet. Cover with a damp towel and let rise until doubled. Bake at 425° for 12–15 minutes.

Makes 1½-2 dozen

# An Unforgettable Tasting Trip

During the 1980s, buying and transporting brandy to Texas was difficult. We needed it to produce our port, which is traditionally made by adding brandy to the fermenting sweet wine, halting fermentation with the alcoholic shock.

Merrill and I had just come from a wonderful port tasting in Boston, where many outstanding Portuguese ports were featured. They allowed our port to be tasted with theirs. I noticed it took quite a while for the brandy to marry with the wine. That was the moment I realized if I could produce the alcohol without the brandy, my port would be smoother. A high alcohol-tolerant yeast strain developed in France gave me the opportunity to test my theory.

We harvested very ripe Lenoir grapes and added the special yeast to the juice each week for 6 weeks, all the while adding fresh juice. At the end of 6 weeks, the alcohol had achieved 19%. That first year's vintage of naturally produced port won a double gold in international competition.

That trip was unforgettable. Only a Texan would think that after a mere 2 years of commercial production, they were ready for international distribution. Upon arrival in Boston, we reported to the convention center to set up our booth. While waiting in line for our passes, we observed the industry giants like Gallo, Mondavi and Brown-Forman were assigned to the fancy hotel suites, while the medium broad-market brands of wines went to the ballroom. We were directed to the basement, lovingly referred to as "The Pit." It seems all unknown wine regions and wineries start in the basement.

To our dismay, we were assigned a booth next to Chateau Ethiopia and Chateau Madrid. The Spaniard was dressed in gold lamé toreador bullfighting garb and smoked 15-inch-long cigars. He was accompanied by two 6-foot flamenco dancers. Between Ethiopian wine and the cigar fog, Paul and I spent 3 days tasting our own wines. Not one person came to visit us. I can only imagine how insulted the Ethiopian and Spanish wineries were to be placed next to a Texas wine!

On the last day of the show, Robert Mondavi and his lovely wife graciously toured The Pit to encourage each winery owner. He stopped and tasted our Messina Hof wines and told us that when our vines were older, our wines would be great. That brief exchange—plus the plethora of photos we took with the Japanese delegation in front of our Texas flag, cowboy boots and hat—made the trip worthwhile. —*Paul*

# Recipes From the Chef's Table

## SHOWCASING TEXAS VINEYARD CUISINE

*"On this mountain the Lord Almighty will prepare a feast of rich food for all peoples, a banquet of aged wine—the best of meats and the finest of wines." Isaiah 25:6 (NIV)*

I t is ironic that the vine marks a beginning and end of human history. Noah planted a vineyard when he landed the ark. The Lord will serve perfect wine at the feast at the end of time.

Paul and I felt honored and blessed to be stewards of a vineyard at this time in Texas wine history, during the late 1980s. Messina Hof was a sculptor in that defining process. We were learning our terroir, experimenting with the grapes and wine styles in multiple regions, and creating food and wine pairings that showcased Texas wine and Texas food—what we coined Texas Vineyard Cuisine.

That sounds as though it would not be difficult or even original, but some of the common concepts of Texas cuisine with Texas wine left us shaking our heads. Time and time again, we were invited to present our wines with "Rattlesnake" this or "Prickly Pear" that. To try to dispel that image, Paul and I hosted many dinners to showcase Messina Hof wines with perfectly paired menus of classic foods with a Texas twist.

In 1996, we opened the Vintage House Restaurant, serving vineyard cuisine inspired by our years of food and wine pairing, trips to Europe, guest chef programs we shared, and the desire to provide that perfect wine and food experience in Texas wine country. Messina Hof Vineyard Cuisine is the expression of the fresh vegetables and herbs grown on the vineyard estate and harvested daily. Messina Hof wines are used in every dish, and each dish is created to perfectly complement a style of wine.

Under the leadership of Executive Chef Ken Ruud, the Vintage House at Messina Hof fulfilled our vision. Chef Ruud and his culinary team developed a Sous Chef program for guests of our Cooking Parties with the Chef. He also transformed the Vintner Dinner experience into a private Chef's Table experience for intimate groups. With his culinary experience in New Orleans and in The Hamptons of New York, he brought a fresh flavor to our Texas Vineyard Cuisine. —*Merrill*

Menu 1

Spicy Calamari

Sicilian Escarole Soup

Osso Buco

Texas Port Tiramisu

# Spicy Calamari

2 cups thinly sliced calamari rings and tentacles
2 cups milk
1 teaspoon black pepper
1 bay leaf
1 cup all-purpose flour
²/₃ cup cornmeal *or* polenta
1 tablespoon blackening spice
2 tablespoons olive oil
2 tablespoons chopped kalamata olives
2 tablespoons grated Parmesan cheese
2 tablespoons chopped fresh parsley
2 teaspoons chili paste with garlic
1 lemon, cut into wedges

Soak calamari in milk with pepper and bay leaf for at least 8 hours; drain. Toss calamari with flour, cornmeal and blackening spice; coat well. Fry in oil until golden brown. Toss with olives, Parmesan cheese, parsley and chili paste. Serve with lemon.

Serves 2

# Sicilian Escarole Soup

½ cup extra virgin olive oil
2 tablespoons chopped shallots
1 cup chopped onion
1 cup chopped pancetta
2 heads escarole, cleaned and coarsely chopped
3 tablespoons chopped garlic
1 cup Messina Hof Private Reserve Chardonnay
1½ gallons chicken stock
2 tablespoons chopped fresh basil
2 tablespoons chopped fresh oregano
2 tablespoons chopped fresh parsley
2 cups white beans, cooked
1 block (5 ounces) Parmesan cheese
Salt and pepper to taste

In a stockpot, heat oil; sauté the shallots, onion and pancetta until onions begin to turn translucent and pancetta begins to get crispy. Add escarole and garlic; sauté for 5 minutes. Add wine, stock, herbs and beans; simmer for 20 minutes. Place the block of cheese in a colander and carefully lower into soup; simmer for 10–15 minutes. Remove cheese and discard. Season soup with salt and pepper.

*Serves 4*

# Osso Buco

½ cup extra virgin olive oil, *divided*

4 veal shanks (2½ to 3 inches thick)

2 cups all-purpose flour

4 ribs celery, diced

2 large carrots, diced

1 large onion, diced

4 tablespoons chopped garlic

1 cup tomato paste

4 cups Messina Hof Merlot

½ gallon veal stock

3 tablespoons chopped fresh oregano

3 tablespoons chopped fresh basil

3 tablespoons chopped fresh parsley

Salt and pepper to taste

In a sauté pan, heat ¼ cup oil. Dredge veal shanks in flour; brown on both sides in oil. Transfer shanks to a deep baking dish. Add remaining oil to sauté pan; sauté celery, carrots, onion and garlic until onions begin to turn translucent. Add tomato paste; sauté for 2–3 minutes. Pour over shanks. Whisk wine into pan drippings, then add to baking dish. Add stock and herbs.

Cover dish with parchment paper and then foil. Bake at 275° for 6 hours or until meat is tender and begins to fall off the bone. Remove shanks and keep warm. Place baking dish on the stove; simmer pan drippings and vegetables. Skim fat. Season with salt and pepper. Return shanks to sauce and serve.

*Serves 4*

## Messina Hof Wines Make Silver Screen Debut

Messina Hof was the first Texas wine featured in a movie. It was the exclusive wine shown in scenes of *The Evening Star*, a 1996 film starring Shirley MacLaine and Jack Nicholson. The movie was a sequel to *Terms of Endearment*, a 1983 film also starring MacLaine and Nicholson. —*Merrill*

# Texas Port Tiramisu

2 cups espresso
1 bottle Messina Hof Papa Paulo Texas Port
2 1/2 cups sugar, *divided*
9 egg yolks
3/4 pound cream cheese, softened
1 vanilla bean, split lengthwise
1 1/2 pounds mascarpone cheese
1 pint heavy whipping cream
90 ladyfingers*
3 cups shaved semisweet chocolate

In a large bowl, combine the espresso, wine and 1 cup sugar; set aside. In a large mixing bowl, whip egg yolks and remaining sugar until light and creamy. Add cream cheese and whip until smooth. Scrape pulp from vanilla bean; add to cream cheese mixture. Fold in mascarpone cheese. Whip cream until stiff peaks form; fold into mascarpone mixture.

Soak ladyfingers, a few at a time, in espresso mixture. Place in a single layer in a 10-inch square pan. Top with a layer of mascarpone mixture and then shaved chocolate. Repeat until pan is filled to the top. Refrigerate for 2 hours before serving.

*The number of ladyfingers needed for this recipe may need to be adjusted, if the ones you are using are much different in size from the ladyfingers we use, which measure 3½ inches long by ¾ inch wide.

Serves 4-6

Menu 2

Sweet Potato-Andouille Soup

Champagne Vinaigrette Salad

Roasted Pork Tenderloin with Roasted
Pineapple, Ginger and Dates

Maple Walnut Torte

# Sweet Potato-Andouille Soup

½ tablespoon olive oil
½ yellow onion, diced
¾ pound andouille sausage, diced
3 sweet potatoes, peeled and diced
4 cups chicken stock
1½ cups heavy whipping cream
½ cup Messina Hof Gewürztraminer
1 cup packed brown sugar
2 tablespoons chopped fresh parsley
2¼ teaspoons black pepper
2¼ teaspoons crushed red pepper
1½ teaspoons ground cinnamon
1½ teaspoons salt

In a stockpot, heat oil; add onion and sausage. Cook for 15–20 minutes. Add sweet potatoes; cook for 15 minutes. Add stock and cream; simmer 20 minutes longer or until potatoes are soft. Cool slightly.

Working in small batches, purée soup in a blender or food processor. Return to the stockpot. Stir in wine. Add brown sugar, parsley, pepper, red pepper, cinnamon and salt, a little at a time, until soup reaches desired level of sweetness. Simmer for 15 minutes or until heated through, stirring often.

Makes 2½ quarts

# Champagne Vinaigrette Salad

3 tablespoons Champagne
2 ½ tablespoons honey
2 tablespoons white vinegar
2 tablespoons Dijon mustard
1 ½ tablespoons chopped fresh parsley
1 tablespoon chopped garlic
1 ½ cups vegetable oil
Mixed salad greens
Dried cranberries, toasted pecans and crumbled
  Gorgonzola

Place the Champagne, honey, vinegar, mustard, parsley and garlic in a blender; while blending on high, slowly drizzle in oil until ingredients are incorporated. Taste and adjust sweetness to your liking. Toss greens with desired amount of vinaigrette; top with cranberries, pecans and Gorgonzola.

Makes 2½ cups

# Roasted Pork Tenderloin with Roasted Pineapple, Ginger and Dates

1 pork tenderloin (³/₄ to 1 pound)

¹/₂ cup olive oil, *divided*

Salt and pepper to taste

2 tablespoons diced pineapple

3 tablespoons grated fresh ginger

2 tablespoons diced dates

2 tablespoons chopped green onions

2 tablespoons minced garlic

¹/₄ cup Messina Hof Pinot Grigio

2 tablespoons chopped fresh parsley

2 tablespoons chopped fresh thyme

2 tablespoons chicken stock

2 tablespoons brown sugar

Brush pork with 2 tablespoons oil; season with salt and pepper. Sear in an ovenproof pan on all sides. Finish in a 350° oven for 15–20 minutes or until a meat thermometer reads 160°. Meanwhile, heat remaining oil in a sauté pan; add pineapple and sauté until browned. Add ginger, dates, onions and garlic; sauté for 2 minutes. Stir in wine, parsley and thyme. Use stock as needed to achieve the right consistency, and add brown sugar, a little at a time, until desired sweetness is met. Slice pork; serve with pineapple mixture.

Serves 2

# Maple Walnut Torte

8 cups chopped walnuts, *divided*
²/₃ cup all-purpose flour
2 teaspoons baking powder
¹/₂ teaspoon salt
10 eggs, *separated*
1¹/₂ cups sugar, *divided*
¹/₄ cup grapeseed *or* vegetable oil
4¹/₂ teaspoons maple syrup, *divided*
3 cups heavy whipping cream
¹/₄ cup confectioners' sugar
8 cups mascarpone cheese

Combine 6 cups walnuts, flour, baking powder and salt; set aside. In a large mixing bowl, whip egg whites with ½ cup sugar until stiff peaks form. In another bowl, beat the egg yolks, oil, remaining sugar and 2 teaspoons syrup. Add nut mixture; mix well. Fold in egg white mixture. Pour into four greased 9-inch cake pans. Bake at 350° for 15–20 minutes. Remove from pans; cool on wire racks.

Whip cream and confectioners' sugar until stiff peaks form. Whip mascarpone with remaining syrup until soft; fold into whipped cream. Spread cream mixture between layers and over top and sides of cake. Sprinkle with remaining walnuts.

Serves 8-10

# VIPs Share Our Passion

As our extended family of Messina Hof grew, we formed a VIP club from our tenured harvest pickers and enthusiastic guests. Called the Red Beret Club in honor of Paul's red beret, each member was presented with a red beret of their own, which they wear with pride. VIPs attend private quarterly parties held in their honor and are included in the annual winemaker's birthday bash and other special events.

The most fulfilling moments of the wine business are when we share the passion we feel for our product and the industry with those who share or appreciate that passion. VIPs radiate passion and remind us of why we make wine. Many of the members volunteer to represent Messina Hof as ambassadors at festivals, vintner's dinners, tastings and group functions. —*Merrill*

## Menu 3

Tomato Herb Butter

Chopped Salad

Striped Bass

Wild Berry Napoleon

# Tomato Herb Butter

1 pound butter, softened
$\frac{1}{2}$ cup all-purpose flour
1$\frac{1}{2}$ teaspoons salt
$\frac{3}{4}$ teaspoon black pepper
$\frac{3}{4}$ teaspoon minced fresh basil
$\frac{3}{4}$ teaspoon minced fresh parsley
$\frac{3}{4}$ teaspoon toasted ground fennel seed
$\frac{1}{4}$ teaspoon ground red pepper
$\frac{1}{4}$ cup crushed tomatoes
Juice of 1 lemon
1$\frac{1}{2}$ teaspoons chopped garlic
$\frac{3}{4}$ teaspoon Worcestershire sauce

In a large mixing bowl, whip butter until smooth. Mix in the flour and seasonings. Add tomatoes, lemon juice, garlic and Worcestershire sauce; whip until completely incorporated. Serve on toast points topped with one boiled shrimp.

Makes 2½ cups

# Chopped Salad

4 cups chopped mixed greens
½ cup diced tomato
½ cup diced carrots
½ cup diced cucumber
½ cup diced roasted peppers
½ cup diced red onion
½ cup diced mozzarella cheese
Paulo Balsamic Vinaigrette (recipe on page 134)
Shredded Parmesan cheese

In a large bowl, combine the greens, vegetables and mozzarella. Toss with vinaigrette and top with Parmesan cheese.

Serves 2-3

# Striped Bass

2 striped bass fillets (8 ounces *each*)
All-purpose flour, salt and pepper
6 tablespoons olive oil
1 cup heavy whipping cream
¼ cup Messina Hof Chardonnay
¼ cup chopped prosciutto
2 tablespoons chopped garlic
2 tablespoons chopped fresh basil

Dredge bass in seasoned flour. Heat oil in an ovenproof pan; brown bass on both sides. Add the remaining ingredients. Finish in a 350° oven for 15–20 minutes or until fish flakes easily with a fork.

Serves 2

# Wild Berry Napoleon

2 cups mascarpone cheese

2 tablespoons heavy whipping cream

$^1/_2$ cup confectioners' sugar

2 vanilla beans, split lengthwise

1 cup *each* fresh strawberries, raspberries and
   blackberries

$^1/_2$ cup sugar

$^1/_2$ yellow sheet cake

In a mixing bowl, whip mascarpone cheese, cream and confectioners' sugar together. Scrape pulp from vanilla beans and add to cheese mixture; set aside. Slice strawberries; toss with raspberries, blackberries and sugar. Cut cake into 3-inch squares. Spread each square with cheese mixture and stack three on top of each other. Place each stack on its side on a plate; cover with berries and serve.

Serves 8

## Texas Chefs Taught Cooking Classes

Requests for group dinners and corporate picnics in the vineyards, and wedding ceremonies and receptions by the lake led to Designer Events, an event planning and production company. Along with private events, Designer Events began a guest chef program. Chefs from all over Texas were invited to stay at Messina Hof and teach a class of food and wine enthusiasts tips to their culinary success.

Classes were held in our home, and each dish was appropriately paired with a Messina Hof wine.

Participating chefs included: Tim Keating, Joe Mannke, Matt Martinez, Rudi Lechner, Carl Walker, Jean Luc Salles, Pamela Manovich, Cheryl Lewis, Klaus Elfeldt, David Frost, Eric Segura, Peter Wabbel, Roger Hyde, Thierry Tellier, Bryan Puckett, Jason Horn, Charlie Watkins and Byron Chargois. —*Merrill*

Crab Pancakes

Tableside Wilted Spinach Salad

Fillets with
Dijon-Peppercorn Pinot Grigio Glaze

Crème Brûlée

# Crab Pancakes

1 pound lump crabmeat

6 eggs

³/₄ cup all-purpose flour

1 cup heavy whipping cream

Juice of 1 lemon

¹/₄ cup chopped green onions

2 tablespoons chopped fresh parsley

1 teaspoon chopped garlic

1 teaspoon Dijon mustard

1 teaspoon Worcestershire sauce

8 to 12 drops hot pepper sauce

3 teaspoons baking powder

¹/₂ teaspoon salt

In a large bowl, mix all ingredients together (should be a loose batter). Pour onto a hot greased griddle and cook as though making pancakes.

Makes 6-8 pancakes

# Tableside Wilted Spinach Salad

6 strips bacon, diced
½ red onion, sliced
8 fresh mushrooms, sliced
2 tablespoons chopped garlic
½ cup Messina Hof Private Reserve Tex-Zin
½ cup packed brown sugar
Salt and pepper to taste
6 cups fresh spinach

In a sauté pan, sauté bacon and onion until bacon is cooked but not crispy and onion is translucent. Add the mushrooms, garlic, wine and brown sugar; cook until wine is bubbling. Season with salt and pepper. Adjust sweetness to your taste. Toss with spinach.

Serves 2

# Fillets with
# Dijon-Peppercorn Pinot Grigio Glaze

*Oven-Roasted Tomatoes*

4 plum tomatoes, cored and quartered

6 tablespoons olive oil, *divided*

2 tablespoons sugar

2 tablespoons chopped fresh basil

2 tablespoons chopped garlic

Salt and pepper to taste

3 tablespoons pine nuts, toasted

*Fillets*

¼ cup olive oil

2 beef tenderloin fillets (4 ounces *each*)

Salt and pepper to taste

*Glaze*

2 tablespoons chopped garlic

2 tablespoons olive oil

½ cup Dijon mustard

⅓ cup Messina Hof Pinot Grigio

1 tablespoon coarsely ground black pepper

1 tablespoon chopped fresh basil

Salt to taste

Toss tomatoes with 4 tablespoons oil, sugar, basil, garlic, salt and pepper. Place in a baking dish. Bake, uncovered, at 300° for 1 hour or until cooked through and dry. Coarsely chop the tomatoes; sauté with pine nuts in remaining oil.

For fillets, in an ovenproof pan, heat oil. Season beef with salt and pepper; brown in oil on both sides. Finish in a 350° oven until meat reaches desired doneness. Meanwhile, for glaze, sauté garlic in oil for 2 minutes. Add the mustard, wine, pepper and basil; simmer for 3 minutes. Season with salt.

To serve, spoon glaze onto plate. Shingle beef over glaze; top with tomato mixture.

Serves 2

# Crème Brûlée

1 quart heavy whipping cream
2 vanilla beans
1 cinnamon stick
12 egg yolks
1 cup sugar

In a saucepan, bring cream, vanilla beans and cinnamon stick to a boil. In a mixing bowl, beat egg yolks and sugar until creamy. Temper with some of the hot cream mixture; stir into the saucepan.

Remove from the heat. Strain and discard vanilla beans and cinnamon stick.

Pour into 9-ounce ramekins. Place in a water bath. Bake at 325° for 20 minutes or until firm. Cool. Caramelize sugar on top. Serve with vanilla whipped cream, fresh strawberries and a chocolate-dipped spoon.

Serves 12

# Basil Prosciutto Crostini

*Balsamic Syrup*

3 cups balsamic vinegar

¼ cup Messina Hof Private Reserve Cabernet

⅔ cup packed brown sugar

*Crostini*

6 thin baguette slices

2 teaspoons basil pesto

6 slices plum tomato

½ cup thinly sliced prosciutto

6 slices fresh mozzarella

2 teaspoons chopped fresh basil

Extra virgin olive oil

For balsamic syrup, combine the vinegar, wine and brown sugar in a saucepan; reduce until thickened. Brush baguette slices with pesto and lightly toast. Top each slice with tomato, prosciutto and mozzarella. Place in oven until cheese is melted. Top with chopped basil. Drizzle with oil and balsamic syrup.

Serves 2

# Crab Avocado Salad

1 cup chopped salad greens
¼ cup cilantro lime vinaigrette
1 cup lump crabmeat
½ cup pico de gallo
1 avocado, peeled, pitted and diced
Corn tortilla strips
Roasted vegetable gazpacho (in squeeze bottle)

Toss greens with half of the vinaigrette and toss crab with the remainder. In two 4-inch rings, layer greens, pico, avocado and crab. Top with tortilla strips; drizzle gazpacho around salad on the plate.

Serves 2

# Macadamia-Crusted Halibut

³/₄ cup olive oil, *divided*
2 halibut fillets (8 ounces *each*)
¹/₂ cup mayonnaise
2 tablespoons Messina Hof Pinot Grigio
¹/₄ cup chopped toasted macadamia nuts
¹/₄ cup diced green onions
3 tablespoons chopped garlic
2 tablespoons grated fresh ginger
1 cup orange marmalade
¹/₂ cup Messina Hof Gewürztraminer
¹/₄ cup orange juice
4 chipotle peppers, chopped

Heat 6 tablespoons oil in an ovenproof pan; brown halibut on both sides. Combine mayonnaise and Pinot Grigio; brush over top of fillets. Cover with nuts. Finish in a 350° oven for 15–20 minutes or until fish flakes easily with a fork.

Meanwhile, in a saucepan, heat remaining oil. Add onions, garlic and ginger; sauté for 2 minutes. Add marmalade, Gewürztraminer, orange juice and peppers; simmer for 15 minutes or until thickened. Serve with halibut.

Serves 2

# Port Zabaglione

6 egg yolks
1 cup sugar, *divided*
¹/₃ cup Messina Hof Ivory Ports of Call
1 cup *each* fresh strawberries, raspberries and
   blackberries

In a double boiler over low heat, whisk the egg yolks with ½ cup sugar until foamy. Add wine, a little at a time, whisking constantly until mixture thickens. Slice strawberries; toss with raspberries, blackberries and remaining sugar. In stemmed wineglasses, layer the custard and berries.

Serves 6

# Recipes From the Wine Cellar

## PERFECT PAIRINGS WITH FOOD

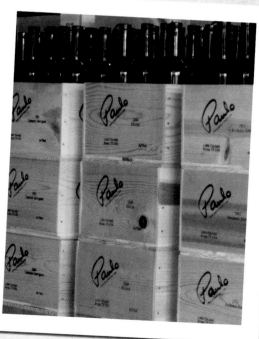

*H*ave you ever eaten a meal where the wine and food were so good that you just couldn't forget about it? Then, did you later have that same wine with a different dish or the same dish with a different wine, only to be disappointed? Count yourself fortunate to have experienced the perfect marriage of wine and food. Each complements or balances the other.

Wine and food of like flavors, textures and tastes marry in great harmony ... or opposites can perfectly complement one another. Balance is the key. Like people, one completes the other.

Most wine lovers choose their wine first and then select the entrée. Wine is the constant of the meal ... food is the variable. We cannot change the wine we select, but we can change the food to enhance the food and wine experience.

Wines should be matched to the strongest flavor on the plate, which is usually the seasonings or sauces. It is no longer the simple "rule" of white wines with white meats and red wines with red meats. Sauces are the true personalities of any dish and the bridge between wine and food. Game meats are the exception, as they have such pronounced flavors.

A natural affinity of flavor occurs by using in the dish the same wine you will serve with the meal. Also, taste the sauce with the wine. Each wine will affect the sauce differently, requiring adjustments in sweetness, acidity and seasonings.

Here are some other hints to help make food and wine pairing simple:

- Mask salty dishes with slightly sweet wines.
- Serve cool, sweet, low-alcohol wines with hot, spicy foods. Higher alcohol content accentuates heat.
- Never use bad wine in cooking. If it tastes too bad to drink, you should put it in the vinegar barrel, not in your food.
- For added flavor, substitute half to three-fourths of the liquid called for in the recipe with wine. The dish will also require less salt.
- When combining sweet wines with desserts, make sure the wine is always sweeter than the dessert.
- When serving wines to a large group whose tastes you don't know, select a light, semi-dry wine like Chenin Blanc, Johannisberg Riesling or Muscat Canelli, or a light, dry Chardonnay with little or no oak or a Pinot Grigio. These wines are most universally enjoyed.
- Choose a wine from the region where you are dining ... when in Texas, drink Texas wine! —*Merrill*

# Wine and Sauce Pairings

### Dry Whites
*Dry white wines tend to pair best with creamy or oil-based sauces and with wine-based sauces of like acidity.*

### Semi-Dry Whites
*Sweeter wines tend to pair best with spicy, hot sauces and with low-fat, more acidic sauces. Be careful pairing with sweet sauces, as the sauce should not be sweeter than the wine. Sauces sweeter than the wine will make sweet wine taste sour and thin.*

### Dry Reds
*Full-bodied red wines are so flavorful that they pair best with more flavorful sauces. Heavier sauces with higher fat content and lower acidity work well with these wines.*

| Dry Whites | Semi-Dry Whites | Dry Reds |
|---|---|---|
| Chardonnay | Blush | Barbera |
| Champagne/Sparkling Wine | Chenin Blanc | Cabernet Franc |
| French Colombard | Gamay Beaujolais | Cabernet Sauvignon |
| Fumé Blanc | Gewürztraminer | Malbec |
| Pinot Grigio/Pinot Gris | Grenache | Merlot |
| Sauvignon Blanc | Muscat Canelli | Nebbiolo |
| Sémillon | Riesling | Pinot Noir |
| Viognier | White Cabernet | Sangiovese |
| | White Merlot | Shiraz |
| | White Zinfandel | Tempranillo |
| | | Zinfandel |

| Dry Whites | Semi-Dry Whites | Dry Reds |
|---|---|---|
| Beurre Blanc | Alfredo | Balsamic Vinaigrette |
| Caper | Barbecue | Béchamel with Parmigiano-Reggiano |
| Dijonnaise | Cajun/Creole | Bolognese |
| Florentine | Cocktail | Creamy Sun-Dried Tomato |
| Green Pesto | Cucumber | Fresh Tomato |
| Herbed Butter | Curry | Gorgonzola Cream |
| Hollandaise | Garlic | Marinara |
| Lemon-Cream Basil | Green Pesto | Mushroom |
| Lemon Mustard | Hot Mustard | Nutmeg Cream |
| Light Gorgonzola | Mexican Tomato | Oil and Parmesan |
| Lobster Cream | Orange Liqueur | Paprika |
| Paprika | Paprika | Roasted Red Pepper |
| Piccata | Primavera | Tomato Cheese |
| Seafood Spaghetti | Sweet-and-Sour | |
| White Onion | Tomato Basil | |

# Natural Flavor Affinities with Wines

When preparing a dish for a particular wine, you can use ingredients that complement and help bridge the food and wine.

These are a few ingredients that I have enjoyed over the years. This can be the starting point for discovering your own favorites.

## White Wines

| | |
|---|---|
| **Chardonnay** | apple, butter, ginger, lemon, melon, mustard seed, orange, peach, pineapple, sage, tarragon |
| **Chenin Blanc** | apple, caper, caraway, cilantro, cucumber, curry, dill, fennel, ginger, lemon, lemon basil, lemon thyme, parsley, pear, tomato |
| **Gewürztraminer** | allspice, almond, cilantro, clove, cumin, curry, garlic, ginger, honey, jasmine, mint, mustard, peppers (spicy), pumpkin, tomato, walnut |
| **Muscat Canelli** | almond, apricot, cardamom, caraway, cinnamon, coconut, cucumber, curry, endive, ginger, lemon verbena, mustard, nutmeg, orange, peach, raisin, sorrel, tomato |
| **Pinot Grigio** | chive, coriander, cucumber, dill, fennel, fig, grapefruit, honey, lemon, melon, olive, orange, papaya, parsley, savory, squash, thyme |
| **Riesling** | apple, cabbage, candied angelica, caraway, cinnamon, coriander, curry, leek, lemon, lemon verbena, mint, mustard, onion, orange, peach, pineapple, saffron, strawberry |
| **Sauvignon Blanc** | almond, basil, bay leaf, bell pepper (red and yellow), chive, cilantro, curry (mild), dill, eggplant, garlic, ginger, grapefruit, hearts of palm, leek, lemon, lemon thyme, marjoram, mushroom, mustard, nutmeg, onion, orange, parsley, pistachio, rosemary, sesame seeds (toasted), sorrel, tarragon, tomato, turmeric |

# Natural Flavor Affinities with Wines
## Pink Wines

**Blush and Light Rosé**  apple, bok choy, cardamom, ginger, greens, juniper berry, nutmeg, orange, raspberry, strawberry

## Red Wines

**Cabernet Franc**  bell pepper (green), black pepper, chocolate, raspberries, rosemary, thyme, wild berries

**Cabernet Sauvignon**  allspice, balsamic reduction, bay leaf, bell pepper (green), blackberry, black currant, black pepper, mace, marjoram, mint, mushroom, nuts, parsley, rosemary, thyme, tomato (roasted), wild rice

**Merlot**  allspice, basil, blackberry, cinnamon, eggplant, elderberry, mace, mint, mushroom, nuts, oregano, peas, peppercorn (green), rosemary, tarragon, thyme, tomato, wild rice

**Pinot Noir**  allspice, balsamic reduction, basil, black cherry, black pepper, cinnamon, clove, mint, nutmeg, orange, pecan, plum, raisin, rosemary, sage, thyme, walnut

**Shiraz**  balsamic reduction, bay leaf, blackberry, cardamom, clove, juniper berry, mace, rosemary, tarragon, white pepper

**Zinfandel**  anise, balsamic reduction, bay leaf, black pepper, cinnamon, clove, eggplant, fennel, juniper berry, mushroom, orange, oregano, raspberry, sage, strawberry, tarragon, thyme

# Pairing Mushrooms with Food and Wine

## Oyster

These delicate mushrooms are best cooked, such as sautéed with butter and onion. They can be substituted for white mushrooms or used along with them. Oyster mushrooms are good in chicken, veal, pork and seafood dishes.

*Best wines:* Johannisberg Riesling, White Zinfandel, Chenin Blanc, Blush

## Enoki

With a mild flavor and light crunch, enoki mushrooms can be served raw in salads, layered in sandwiches and used as a garnish for appetizers, soups and entrées. Trim the roots of these delicate mushrooms at the base of the cluster and separate the stems before serving.

*Best wines:* Sauvignon Blanc, Gamay Beaujolais, Gewürztraminer, Muscat Canelli, Pinot Grigio

## White (Button)

The most common of the mushrooms, these have a firm texture. Serve whole or sliced raw white mushrooms in hors d'oeuvres, salads and veggie trays ... or roast or sauté with minced garlic and thyme as a side dish.

*Best wines:* Chardonnay, Pinot Noir, Gamay Beaujolais, Gewürztraminer, Muscat Canelli, Pinot Grigio

## Crimini

With an earthy flavor and firm texture, these mushrooms pair well with beef, wild game and vegetable dishes. Serve criminis raw or cooked, such as sautéed in butter, garlic, oregano, salt and pepper.

*Best wines:* Chardonnay, Pinot Noir, Sauvignon Blanc, Gamay Beaujolais, Gewürztraminer, Pinot Grigio

## Shittake

These meaty mushrooms are delicious in a variety of stir-frys, pasta dishes, soups and entrées. Shiitakes are suitable for almost any cooking method, including sautéing, baking and broiling. The tough, woody stems should be removed, but they can be used to flavor stocks and soups.

*Best wines:* Paulo, Shiraz, Cabernet Franc, Pinot Noir, Cabin Noir

## Portobello

The popularity of the portobello burger is a tip-off to this mushroom's meaty flavor. This versatile, firm mushroom can be also stuffed and served whole ... grilled, baked or deep-fried ... or sliced and added to stir-frys and sauces.

*Best wines:* Paulo, Cabernet Sauvignon, Merlot, Tex-Zin, Cabernet Franc

# Chipotle Stuffed Crimini

*Served with Messina Hof Gewürztraminer*

3 tablespoons chopped roasted garlic
2 tablespoons chopped chipotle peppers
2 tablespoons diced sun-dried tomatoes
2 tablespoons oyster sauce
1 cup puréed roasted peppers
1/2 cup heavy whipping cream
1/4 cup Messina Hof Gewürztraminer
Salt and pepper to taste
4 squares puff pastry (5 inches *each*)
4 fresh crimini mushrooms
1 egg, beaten

In a sauté pan, cook the garlic, chipotle peppers, tomatoes and oyster sauce until combined; set aside. In another pan, reduce roasted peppers, cream and wine until mixture reaches desired thickness. Season with salt and pepper; keep warm.

Roll out pastry squares; top each with one mushroom, cap side down. Spoon chipotle mixture onto mushrooms; completely enclose with pastry. Place on a baking sheet. Brush with egg. Bake at 350° for 10–15 minutes or until golden brown.

*Serves 4*

# Corn and Clam Bisque

*Served with Messina Hof Sauvignon Blanc*

1/4 cup diced shallots
4 strips bacon, diced
1 teaspoon all-purpose flour
1/2 cup heavy whipping cream
1/4 cup milk
8 littleneck clams, chopped
1/2 cup clam juice
1/2 cup fresh corn
2 tablespoons Messina Hof Sauvignon Blanc
4 dashes hot pepper sauce
1/4 teaspoon white pepper

In a saucepan, cook shallots and bacon until crisp; remove and set aside. Add flour to drippings; cook and stir over medium heat until mixture bubbles. Slowly whisk in cream and milk, stirring constantly. Bring to a boil; reduce heat to a low simmer. Add remaining ingredients. Return shallots and bacon to the pan. Simmer for 10 minutes or until heated through.

*Serves 2*

# Cactus Pear Corn Pancakes

*Served with Messina Hof Angel Riesling*

2 ¹/₂ cups cactus pear juice
¹/₂ cup lemon juice
¹/₂ cup Messina Hof Angel Riesling
3 cups sugar
Cornstarch
1 cup yellow cornmeal
1 cup all-purpose flour
1 tablespoon baking powder
¹/₂ teaspoon salt
1¹/₂ cups milk
2 eggs
6 tablespoons butter, melted

For syrup, combine the pear juice, lemon juice, wine and sugar in a saucepan. Bring to a boil; reduce to a simmer. Cook until sugar is dissolved. Adjust sweetness; thicken with cornstarch until syrup reaches desired thickness.

For pancakes, in a mixing bowl, combine the cornmeal, flour, baking powder and salt. Whisk in milk and eggs until blended, then whisk in butter. Cook on a hot greased griddle until golden brown on both sides. Serve with cactus pear syrup and pico de gallo if desired.

Makes 10 pancakes and 5 cups syrup

# Lemongrass Salad

*Served with Messina Hof Muscat Canelli*

2 stalks lemongrass, grated
1 cup water
1 cup sugar
¼ cup Messina Hof Muscat Canelli
2 tablespoons chopped shallots
1 tablespoon rice wine vinegar
1 teaspoon sesame seeds
¼ cup salad oil
3 cups mixed greens
3 spring roll wrappers, fried
5 tablespoons diced red bell peppers
5 tablespoons diced scallions
5 tablespoons diced pineapple

For the vinaigrette, combine the lemongrass, water and sugar in a saucepan. Bring to a boil; cool. Transfer to a food processor or blender; add the wine, shallots, vinegar and sesame seeds. While blending, slowly drizzle in oil. Toss greens with ¼ cup vinaigrette; place on salad plates. Arrange spring roll wrappers, red peppers, scallions and pineapple over greens.

Serves 2

# Pan-Roasted Grouper in Orange-Soy Glaze

*Served with Messina Hof Chenin Blanc*

1 cup soy sauce
½ cup Messina Hof Chenin Blanc
1 teaspoon minced garlic
1 teaspoon minced ginger
½ cup orange juice
⅓ cup honey
Cornstarch and cold water
2 tablespoons olive oil
6 grouper fillets (7 to 8 ounces *each*)

For glaze, combine the soy sauce, wine, garlic, ginger, orange juice and honey in a saucepan; simmer for about 10 minutes. Thicken with cornstarch and water as needed. Heat oil in an ovenproof sauté pan; sear grouper on both sides. Finish in a 350° oven for 5 minutes. Top with glaze. Sprinkle with black and white sesame seeds if desired.

Serves 6

# Shrimp Scampi Linguine

*Served with Messina Hof Sauvignon Blanc*

8 ounces uncooked linguine
¼ cup olive oil
4 tablespoons chopped shallots
2 tablespoons chopped garlic
10 shrimp (16/20 size)
1 cup diced tomatoes
1 cup Messina Hof Sauvignon Blanc
2 tablespoons lemon juice
6 tablespoons chopped fresh basil
Salt and pepper to taste
3 tablespoons cold butter

Shredded Parmesan cheese
Chopped fresh parsley

Cook linguine according to package directions. Meanwhile, heat oil in a sauté pan; sauté shallots and garlic until garlic begins to brown. Add shrimp and tomatoes; sauté for a few minutes. Add wine and lemon juice; cook until shrimp turn pink. Add basil, salt and pepper. Mound with cold butter. Drain linguine; toss with shrimp mixture. Top with Parmesan cheese and parsley.

Serves 2

# Pan-Roasted Salmon
# with Lemon-Chive Beurre Blanc

*Served with Messina Hof Sauvignon Blanc*

1 cup Messina Hof Sauvignon Blanc
$^1/_2$ cup lemon juice
1 teaspoon lemon zest
1 clove garlic, peeled
1 bay leaf
2 cups heavy whipping cream
$^1/_2$ pound cold butter, cubed
$^1/_2$ cup chopped fresh chives
1 tablespoon grapeseed oil
2 salmon fillets (7 to 8 ounces *each*)

In a saucepan, combine the wine, lemon juice and zest, garlic, bay leaf and cream. Cook until reduced by one-third. Slowly add butter, a little at a time, until incorporated. Discard garlic and bay leaf. Stir in chives; keep warm.

In an ovenproof sauté pan, heat oil; sear salmon on both sides. Finish in a 350° oven for 10 minutes or until salmon is cooked to desired doneness. Serve with lemon-chive beurre blanc.

Serves 2

*"Cooking and eating should be fun. Every meal at our home is a feast. What is a feast? Simply good food, good wine and good company. When preparing a meal, I always select the wines first and then the menu. This book was done for those who, like me, first pour a glass of wine."* —Merrill

# Steamed Mussels

*Served with Messina Hof Private Reserve Chardonnay*

½ cup olive oil
¼ cup diced shallots
3 teaspoons chopped garlic
5 cups cleaned mussels
1½ cups Messina Hof Private Reserve Chardonnay
¼ cup chopped fresh parsley
3 teaspoons chopped fresh basil
5 tablespoons cold butter

In a sauté pan, heat oil. Add shallots and garlic; sauté for 2 minutes. Add mussels, wine, parsley, basil and butter; cover and steam until mussels open.

Serves 2

# Duck Breast Dewberry

*Served with Messina Hof Shiraz*

2 duck breasts (6 to 8 ounces *each*), skin on
$^1\!/_2$ cup dewberries with juice
$^1\!/_2$ cup Messina Hof Shiraz
1 sprig fresh rosemary
3 tablespoons brown sugar

Score the duck skin and place skin side down in a hot ovenproof sauté pan; sear until golden brown. Turn and brown the other side. Turn over again so the skin side is down. Bake at 350° until meat reaches desired doneness, about 10 minutes for medium-rare. Remove duck; keep warm. Add the remaining ingredients to pan; simmer for 2–3 minutes. Spoon sauce onto plates. Slice duck breasts as thin as possible and fan out over sauce.

Serves 2

# Porterhouse Steak with Roasted Tomato and Rosemary Sauce

*Served with Messina Hof Paulo Meritage*

3 plum tomatoes, cored and halved
¹/₂ cup olive oil, *divided*
6 tablespoons sugar
4 tablespoons chopped fresh basil
6 tablespoons chopped garlic, *divided*
Salt and pepper to taste
¹/₄ cup sliced shallots
3 tablespoons chopped fresh rosemary
1 cup Messina Hof Paulo Meritage
2 beef porterhouse steaks (14 ounces *each*)

In a bowl, combine the tomatoes, ¼ cup oil, sugar, basil, 2 tablespoons garlic, salt and pepper. Transfer to a baking dish. Bake, uncovered, at 300° for 3 hours (tomatoes should be shriveled but not burned).

In a sauté pan, heat 2 tablespoons oil. Add shallots and sauté until golden brown. Add rosemary, 1 tablespoon garlic and roasted tomato mixture; sauté for 2 minutes. Add wine and cook until reduced. Meanwhile, rub steaks with salt, pepper and remaining garlic. In an ovenproof pan, sear steaks in remaining oil until browned on both sides. Finish in a 350° oven for 15 minutes or until meat reaches desired doneness. Serve with roasted tomato sauce.

Serves 2

# Grilled Texas Strip Steak with Paulo Red Onion Marmalade

*Served with Messina Hof Paulo Cabernet Sauvignon*

2 strip steaks (10 ounces *each*)
6 cloves garlic, crushed, *divided*
3 sprigs fresh rosemary, *divided*
10 tablespoons olive oil, *divided*
Salt and pepper to taste
1 red onion
2 shallots, chopped
3 cups red wine vinegar
$\frac{1}{2}$ cup Messina Hof Paulo Cabernet Sauvignon
6 tablespoons corn syrup
2 tablespoons brown sugar

Place the steaks in a bowl; add 3 crushed garlic cloves, 1 sprig of rosemary (pulled apart) and 6 tablespoons oil. Sprinkle with salt and pepper; let stand while preparing marmalade.

Slice onion in half, then thinly slice from one end to the other; set aside. In a saucepan, heat the remaining oil. Sauté shallots and remaining garlic for 2 minutes, being careful not to burn. Add onion; sauté until soft and translucent. Add vinegar, wine, remaining rosemary sprigs (whole) and corn syrup; simmer until mixture reduces and starts to thicken. Add brown sugar and stir until dissolved. Remove rosemary sprigs. Season with salt and pepper.

Place steaks on a hot grill on a diagonal; grill for 3 minutes. Turn steaks on a diagonal in the other direction; grill for 3 minutes. Flip steaks over and repeat. Cook until meat reaches desired doneness. Top with red onion marmalade.

Serves 2

# Strawberries Romanoff

*Served with Messina Hof Tawny Port*

3 tablespoons butter
$1/2$ lemon
$1/2$ orange
4 tablespoons orange liqueur
4 tablespoons banana liqueur
3 tablespoons brown sugar
$3/4$ cup sliced fresh strawberries
2 tablespoons Messina Hof Tawny Port
2 tablespoons rum
Ice cream

After turning on the burner, melt butter in a sauté pan. Squeeze the lemon and orange into the pan; add the liqueurs. Cook until juices are reduced by half. Add the brown sugar and strawberries; stir and wait while the substance caramelizes. Once caramelized, add wine.

When mixture looks ready and thick, pull the pan halfway off the burner and tilt just a bit so the bottom rim of the pan is in the flame heating up. Once the pan is very hot, pour the rum on the inside rim of the pan. Carefully pull the pan back into the flame while just tipping it a bit to catch the rum to the flame, and it will then ignite and FLAME! Serve over ice cream.

Serves 2

# Cherries Jubilee

*Served with Messina Hof Papa Paulo Port*

3 tablespoons butter
¹/₂ lemon
4 tablespoons orange liqueur
3 tablespoons brown sugar
3 tablespoons Messina Hof Port Fudge
2 tablespoons Messina Hof Papa Paulo Port
³/₄ cup dark pitted cherries
2 tablespoons rum
Ice cream

After turning on the burner, melt butter in a sauté pan. Squeeze the lemon into the pan; add liqueur. Cook until juices are reduced by half. Add brown sugar; stir and wait while the substance caramelizes. Once caramelized, add the fudge and let it melt. Once melted, add wine. When the substance is caramelized and thick, add the cherries. (The cherries do not need to be in the pan for long or they will get too soft.)

When mixture looks ready and thick, pull the pan halfway off the burner and tilt just a bit so the bottom rim of the pan is in the flame heating up. Once the pan is very hot, pour the rum on the inside rim of the pan. Carefully pull the pan back into the flame while just tipping it a bit to catch the rum to the flame, and it will then ignite and FLAME! Serve over ice cream.

Serves 2

# Chocolate and Wine ... Like Love and Marriage

Chocolate and wine go together like love and marriage. And for some, the combination is just pure ecstasy. Like great wine, great chocolate not only tastes good but appeals to all of the senses with complex aromas, rich layers of flavors and textures, distinct personalities of style and wonderfully lingering aftertastes.

What is fermented ... typically described in terms of fruits, spices, herbs and vegetables ... has hundreds of distinct aromas ... and is blended by a master? Most would answer wine. That is correct, but so is chocolate. Amazingly, chocolate can have many different aromas, from citrus and cherry to bell pepper, grass and cedar. These are the same descriptors used for wine. Good chocolate needs acid balance the same as good wine does.

No wonder wine and chocolate are so well suited. And, with so many different chocolates and wines to choose from, pairings are limitless. The perfect pairing of wine and chocolate comes in the balance of flavor and texture in the mouth. This is called the "weight" of the chocolate or wine. If the chocolate has a heavy weight, meaning bold dark flavors with rich texture, then it demands a bold, dark red wine like port.

Port is, of course, the classic pairing and one that can rarely go wrong. At Messina Hof, we produce six different ports. Our Paulo Port, Private Reserve Papa Paulo Port and Barrel Reserve Papa Paulo Port are ideal with dark chocolate. Each year Messina Hof celebrates the marriage of port and chocolate by creating an entire menu of courses containing chocolate and served with port.

There are other marriages that work as well and offer a fun challenge in pushing the envelope of new flavor combinations. If you have a heavy-weighted bitter chocolate, try Merlot, Cabernet Sauvignon, Shiraz or Cabernet Franc. Yes, you can pair dry reds with chocolate. Dark chocolate has the highest cocoa content and therefore the boldest flavors, which complement the bold flavors of dark red wines.

Add a little spicy pepper or some rich roasted nuts to the mix, and try a big Zinfandel. Dried cherries and raw nuts can yield a Pinot Noir-friendly chocolate.

Milk chocolate is lighter and more delicate. It has creamier, lighter chocolate flavors, which are medium in weight. These chocolates are usually sweeter and go better with lighter and sweeter wines. Light ports, like the Messina Hof Ebony, and really smooth Tawny ports pair well. In addition, try a sweet Riesling, Muscat Canelli or Chenin Blanc with milk chocolate.

White chocolate is sometimes rejected by chocoholics who think it is not chocolate. It is made of cocoa butter with milk and sugar. Usually the sweetest of the chocolate family, it has the lightest weight of all. Late harvest wines and white ports, like the Messina Hof Ivory, are natural mates for this family member.

The goal is to make both the wine and chocolate shine, for each to bring out the best in the other.
—*Merrill*

# Hearts of Cream

*Served with Messina Hof Ivory Ports of Call*

1 pound rich cream cheese, softened
2 tablespoons heavy whipping cream
⅛ teaspoon salt
¾ cup sugar, *divided*
1 cup whipped cream
½ cup water
2 cups fresh red and black raspberries
Juice of ½ lemon
¼ cup Messina Hof Ivory Ports of Call
1 tablespoon chocolate fudge, melted
12 rose petals, washed

In a large mixing bowl, beat cream cheese, cream, salt and ¼ cup sugar until smooth. Fold into the whipped cream. Pour into oiled heart-shaped custard cups or molds. Chill overnight or until firm.

In a saucepan, bring water and remaining sugar to a boil. Simmer, stirring occasionally, for 5 minutes or until mixture reaches the consistency of syrup. Add raspberries; cool. Stir in lemon juice, wine and fudge. Unmold hearts of cream; top with chocolate raspberry sauce and sprinkle with rose petals.

Serves 2

119

# Chocolate Praline Pie

*Served with Messina Hof Private Reserve Papa Paulo Port*

3³/₄ cups chopped semisweet chocolate
2 cups butter
2 cups heavy whipping cream
8 egg yolks
1¹/₂ cups confectioners' sugar
³/₄ cup Messina Hof Private Reserve Papa Paulo Port
2 cups chopped pecans
2 pastry shells (9 inches), baked

In a double boiler, melt chocolate and butter with cream. Whisk eggs and slowly add to chocolate mixture, whisking constantly. Whisk in the confectioners' sugar and wine. Add pecans. Pour into pastry shells. Cool. Garnish with strawberries and whipped cream.

Makes 2 pies

## *Have Fun with Wine Tasting at Home*

When planning a home wine-tasting party, first select a theme:

*Horizontal Tasting*—wines from the same region, variety and vintage, but from different wineries.

*Vertical Tasting*—wines from the same winery and variety, but different vintages.

*Regional Tasting*—wines from the same variety and vintage, but from different regions.

*Wine Tasting Game*—choose five different wines and have a blind tasting to identify the label or guess the variety.

Then select the tasting procedure and create rating sheets and handouts.

Other supplies you'll need are wineglasses, dump buckets, corkscrews and palate cleansers (such as bread and cheese). If doing a blind tasting, mask the wine bottles in brown paper bags before guests arrive.

Prepare a tasting area with a white tablecloth, good lighting and a water pitcher for rinsing. Place enough glasses at each setting so each guest can have all wines for each comparative flight poured simultaneously.

Appoint someone who's knowledgeable about wines to show guests how to rate the wines and act as discussion leader. After each flight has been rated, the leader should open the conversation about each wine and get each guest's input. Following the discussion, the host can reveal the wines and give guests enough time to record the label information. —*Merrill*

# White Chocolate Raspberry Bread Pudding

*Served with Messina Hof Angel Riesling*

18 egg yolks
2 ¼ cups sugar
4 ½ cups milk
4 ½ cups heavy whipping cream
1 ¼ pounds white chocolate, chopped
½ cup Messina Hof Angel Riesling
1 ½ teaspoons vanilla extract
2 ¼ pounds bread, cubed
2 cups fresh raspberries
*Garnish*
1 cup sugar
Vanilla ice cream

In a large mixing bowl, whip egg yolks and sugar until creamy. In a saucepan, bring milk and cream to a boil. Temper egg mixture with cream. Add chocolate, wine and vanilla; mix until incorporated. Toss with bread cubes and raspberries.

Spoon into greased 6-ounce ramekins. Bake at 350° for 45 minutes. Meanwhile, for caramel decorations, heat sugar in a saucepan over medium heat until it liquefies and becomes amber-colored. Cool for a few minutes. On a sheet of waxed paper, drizzle caramel back and forth or in a circular motion, making desired shapes. Cool.

Remove bread pudding from ramekins; top each with a scoop of ice cream and a caramel decoration.

Serves 11

# Wine Serving Tips

Too often at home and in restaurants, wine is served at the improper temperatures. Red wines should be served at 65°F. In hot climates like Texas, room temperature is often warmer than 65°, so in summertime, I usually put my red wines in the refrigerator for 30 minutes prior to serving. This cools the wine to the proper temperature. Red wines are often served too warm, making the alcohol "hot" and the fruit muted.

White wines should be served chilled at a temperature of 45–55°F. If they are served warm, they tend to taste dull and less fruitful. If served too cold, the fruit and bouquet are inhibited. For more formal occasions, use a pre-chilled wine bucket—it makes serving easy, and your guests will appreciate having wine at the right temperature.

There are many different corkscrews in the market today. Choose one that's easy for you to use; don't rely on clever packaging when making your choice. After you have opened your wine, smell the cork; it should smell like wine. Taste the wine before serving.

If the wine is older, there is a possibility that some sediment will develop on the bottom of the bottle; therefore, try not to shake the bottle. Decant the wine, or if you don't have a decanter, carefully pour it to prevent sediment from going into the glass.

Serve yourself before your guests so that any excess cork that has fallen into the bottle will not be poured into your guests' glasses.

When serving multiple wines in one meal, follow these general guidelines:

- *Young before old.* Young wines should be simple and refreshing, preparing the palate for more complex, older wines.
- *White before red.* If a delicate white wine would follow a stronger red, the flavor would be quite bland. Whites are also higher in acid, which helps to stimulate the palate, so when you begin tasting reds, you are ready for the robust flavors.
- *Light-bodied before full-bodied.* For example, with whites, you should taste Pinot Grigio before oak-aged Chardonnay; with reds, taste Pinot Noir before Cabernet Sauvignon and un-oaked wines before oak-aged wines.
- *Dry before sweet.* Dry (meaning absence of sugar) usually connotes wines of higher acidity or tartness. If you serve a sweet wine and follow it with a dry wine, the palate will be jolted. A dry wine, with a noticeable acidity level, cannot compete with the lusciousness or fullness of a sweet wine, so it will seem sour and thin by comparison. —Merrill

# Wine and Cheese Pairings

Since wine and cheese are the most common wine and food combinations for entertainment, here are some suggestions on what to offer. Having different cheeses available with different wines is a fun way for guests to taste something new and learn about the origins of each variety.

| With Dry Whites | With Semi-Dry Whites and Blush | With Dry Reds | With Dessert Wines |
|---|---|---|---|
| Brie (young) | Chèvre | Asiago | Danish Blue |
| Camembert | Edam | Brie (ripe) | Deep Ellum Blue |
| Chèvre | Feta | Cheddar | Cabrales |
| Dry Jack | Gjetost | Chèvre | Fourme d'Ambert |
| Emmental | Limburger | Gorgonzola | Gorgonzola |
| Fontina | Livarot | Herb Caciotta | Mascarpone |
| Gruyère | Monterey Jack | Parmesan | Perail |
| Jarlsberg | Muenster | Provolone (aged) | Roquefort |
| Havarti | Mysost | Montasio | Stilton |
| Herb Caciotta (basil) | Pepper Jack | Romano | Wensleydale |
| Mozzarella | Queso Blanco | Smoked Gouda | |
| Swiss | Queso Fresco | Smoked Gruyère | |

# Recipes From the Heart of the Home

## TOGETHERNESS BEGINS IN THE KITCHEN

When two people become one, a new family is born. Traditions of each are blended into new proprietary traditions like a fine Meritage wine. Each new family is built upon cornerstones ... ours were family, tradition and romance. The foundation of those cornerstones was faith ... faith in the Lord Jesus Christ and faith that whatever we pursued would be in His plan.

The vineyard itself provided guidance. Viticulture and enology flow from the vine and the timing of nature. When the vine is ready, then we do what is needed. We were the vine-tenders of the vineyard as

the Lord was our vine-tender. We learned so many lessons and experienced so much pruning.

In John 15, we learn everything we need to know about growing grapes and also about how we are to love one another and produce good fruits. Vine-tenders prune. When we are pruned, we are made better. *"He cuts off every branch in me that bears no fruit, while every branch that does bear fruit He prunes so that it will be even more fruitful." John 15:2 (NIV)*

Through it all, the time we shared in the kitchen and around the dinner table was what we most enjoyed and cherished. This is where traditions are created, celebrations enjoyed and values shared. —*Merrill*

# Dipping Oil Seasoning

*Paul and I spent hours in the kitchen. It was the place where we could talk and laugh and create together. We tasted everything, even olive oil. Olive oils are like fine wines. After doing a blind tasting of oil from Tunisia, Lebanon, Syria, Greece, Turkey, Spain and Italy, we chose Turkey by far as our favorite olive oil and have used it exclusively ever since. Instead of butter on the table, we use spiced dipping oil for our bread.*

1 tablespoon dried thyme
1 tablespoon paprika
1 teaspoon garlic powder
1 teaspoon onion powder
1 teaspoon salt
¼ teaspoon black pepper
Pinch cayenne pepper

Place all ingredients in a food processor; purée until smooth. For a more fiery batch, double or triple the cayenne. Put 1 teaspoon of seasoning into a small bowl; add enough olive oil to cover. For extra zing, add a splash of balsamic vinegar.

Makes about ¼ cup

# Vintage House Focaccia Bread

1 ounce active dry yeast

3 cups warm water

¹/₂ cup honey

¹/₂ cup olive oil

²/₃ cup chopped fresh rosemary

1¹/₂ tablespoons salt

3¹/₂ pounds bread flour *or* all-purpose flour

In a mixing bowl, dissolve yeast in water; let stand for a few minutes. Add honey and oil; let stand until yeast starts to foam. Add rosemary and salt. Slowly add flour. Dough should be soft and elastic; add additional water or flour, a little at a time, until you've reached the right consistency.

Transfer dough to an oiled bowl; brush oil on top of dough. Cover with plastic wrap and place in a warm area. Once dough has risen to double its size, remove from bowl and roll into desired shapes, working with a small amount of dough at a time.

Wrap again with plastic wrap and place in a warm place. Once dough has risen to almost twice its size, place on a baking sheet. Bake at 350° until golden brown. Brush with oil. Serve warm or allow to cool.

*Serves 12-16*

## Texans Knighted to the Vine

In 1989, Gaye and Arthur Platt came into our lives and introduced us to the Knights of the Vine, a social wine organization in Houston. Gaye was the Lady Master Commander. She and Arthur took on the mantle of Texas wines and carried them all around the world to the KOV Assemblages.

Paul and I were knighted Supreme Master Knight and Supreme Master Lady of the Society. Paul VII was knighted Squire.

Gaye and Arthur supported every Texas wine event. I'll never forget when Paul was on a panel discussing Sauvignon Blanc. He felt that he had just made the best one of his life when Arthur stood up and proudly said it reminded him of a petroleum product. Arthur taught us humility.

The KOV was the first organization in the state of Texas to create an educational fund for viticulture at Texas A&M University. —*Merrill*

# Messina Hof Beggar's Purses

*I'll never forget when Paul and I first took our concept for creating a wine country destination to the bank for funding. After we proudly detailed our business plan to the bankers, they congratulated us, told us it was a novel idea and said we should self-finance it. Then they stood, smiled and shook our hands as they escorted us out the door.*

*Paul turned to me, said the meeting seemed to go well and asked me what kind of financing "self" was. I told him it was time to get out our piggy banks and start counting. Everything was pay as you go. Thank goodness our parents taught us that if we did not have the money in our pockets, we could not afford it.*

*These "beggar's purses" make nice appetizers, and they're also a pretty plate garnish or addition to a salad.*

Phyllo dough pastry sheets
5 tablespoons butter, *divided*
3 tablespoons all-purpose flour
1/2 teaspoon salt
1/8 teaspoon cayenne pepper
1 1/2 cups heavy whipping cream
1/4 cup Messina Hof Chardonnay
1 cup mascarpone cheese
1/2 pound cooked shrimp, halved lengthwise
1/2 cup cooked flaked crabmeat

Cut pastry sheets into 32 4-inch squares; cover with a damp cloth to keep moist. In a saucepan over medium-low heat, melt 3 tablespoons butter. Stir in flour, salt and cayenne; cook and stir until bubbly. Add cream and wine; stir until thickened and smooth. Mix in cheese and seafood; cool.

Put 1 tablespoon of filling in the middle of each pastry square. Moisten edges with water; gather edges over filling and twist top to create a closed purse shape. Place on baking sheets. Bake at 350° for 15–20 minutes or until pastry is golden brown and crisp.

Makes 32 appetizers

# Messina Hof's Vineyard Salad

*Paulo Balsamic Vinaigrette*

1½ cups balsamic vinegar

1 cup Messina Hof Papa Paulo Port

Juice of 1 orange

¼ cup Dijon mustard

¼ cup sugar

1 tablespoon hot pepper sauce

1 tablespoon Worcestershire sauce

1 tablespoon minced garlic

¾ teaspoon black pepper

¼ teaspoon dried oregano

¼ teaspoon salt

5 cups olive oil

*Salad*

1 large portobello mushroom cap

1 red bell pepper

8 asparagus spears

Olive oil

4 to 6 cups torn mixed salad greens

8 ounces crumbled goat cheese

In a bowl, whisk the first 11 vinaigrette ingredients. Slowly add oil, whisking constantly. Set aside.

Brush the mushroom, red pepper and asparagus with oil. Grill mushroom until soft; cool and thinly slice. Char outside of pepper on the grill. Place in a bowl and cover with plastic wrap; let stand for 10–15 minutes. Peel off pepper skin; remove seeds and core. Rinse pepper under cool water and thinly slice. Grill asparagus until tender.

Toss greens with desired amount of vinaigrette; divide among salad plates. Arrange mushroom slices, red pepper slices, asparagus and goat cheese over greens.

Serves 4

# Fennel-Cumin Crusted Scallops with Mango Chutney

*We would often celebrate each Friday with a special candlelight meal. It's easy to let the worries and tests of the day dampen the joy of family life. We learned to focus on the blessings of the week. Burdens that seemed so heavy were lifted from our lives. "Cast your burdens on the Lord and He shall sustain you." Psalm 55:22 (NIV)*

*Chutney*

¼ cup diced green onions

¼ cup diced red onion

1 tablespoon minced garlic

1 tablespoon olive oil

2 mangoes, peeled and diced

¼ cup diced bell pepper

¼ cup Messina Hof Pinot Grigio

¼ cup white vinegar

2 tablespoons brown sugar

*Scallops*

4 tablespoons fennel seed, toasted

3 teaspoons ground cumin

2 teaspoons brown sugar

8 pomegranates

½ bottle Messina Hof Papa Paulo Port

2 cups sugar

1 lemon quarter

¼ cup olive oil

10 large scallops

In a saucepan, sauté onions and garlic in oil until translucent. Add remaining chutney ingredients; simmer for about 15 minutes, stirring occasionally.

Meanwhile, grind toasted fennel with cumin and brown sugar; set aside. Scrape seeds and juice from pomegranates into a saucepan; add port and sugar. Squeeze lemon into the mixture. Simmer for 20 minutes. Purée and strain. Return to the heat; adjust seasoning and thickness as desired.

Heat oil in a sauté pan. Dredge scallops in cumin-fennel mixture; brown in oil on both sides. Serve scallops with mango chutney. Drizzle pomegranate sauce around edge of plates.

Serves 2

# Lobster Rockefeller

2 lobster tails in shell (12 ounces *each*)
4 cups water
1¼ cups Messina Hof Chardonnay
1 cup lemon juice
2 tablespoons chopped fresh spinach
1 tablespoon chopped shallots
1¼ cups heavy whipping cream
Salt and pepper to taste
2 tablespoons hollandaise sauce
2 tablespoons seasoned breadcrumbs

In a large pot, poach lobster tails in water, wine and lemon juice for about 8 minutes. Meanwhile, in a small saucepan, cook spinach and shallots in cream until thickened. Season with salt and pepper. Crack lobster tails to expose all meat. Top with spinach mixture and drizzle with hollandaise. Broil for about 2 minutes to brown. Finish with breadcrumbs.

Serves 2

# Tex-Zin BBQ Turkey

*BBQ Sauce*
³/₄ cup diced onion
¹/₂ tablespoon sesame oil
2 teaspoons grated fresh ginger
³/₄ cup orange juice
¹/₂ cup honey
¹/₄ cup balsamic vinegar
¹/₂ cup hoisin sauce
¹/₃ cup Worcestershire sauce
¹/₃ cup soy sauce
6 tablespoons brown sugar
3 tablespoons Messina Hof Private Reserve Tex-Zin
3 tablespoons tomato juice
2 tablespoons Dijon mustard
1 tablespoon minced lemongrass
2 teaspoons minced fresh cilantro
¹/₂ teaspoon paprika
¹/₂ teaspoon salt
¹/₄ teaspoon black pepper

*Grilled Pineapple Salsa*
¹/₄ fresh pineapple, sliced
1 tablespoon grapeseed oil
¹/₂ cup diced red bell pepper
¹/₄ cup diced red onion
¹/₄ cup diced green onions
Juice of 1 lime
1 tablespoon minced fresh cilantro
1 teaspoon salt
2 tablespoons brown sugar

1 turkey (12 to 14 pounds)

In a saucepan, sauté onion in sesame oil until translucent. Add ginger and cook for 3 minutes. Stir in the remaining sauce ingredients. Cook for 15–20 minutes. Strain sauce and cook until thickened. Cool.

Brush pineapple slices with grapeseed oil. Grill until soft. Dice pineapple; mix with the remaining salsa ingredients. Let stand for at least 30 minutes.

Grill turkey over medium indirect heat for 3–4 hours or until a meat thermometer reads 180°, brushing occasionally with BBQ sauce. Slice turkey; drizzle with any remaining BBQ sauce. Serve with pineapple salsa. (Turkey may be baked at 325° instead of grilled.)

Serves 8-10

# Mini Beef Wellingtons

36 whole garlic cloves, peeled
$\frac{1}{2}$ cup olive oil, *divided*
2 beef fillets (4 ounces *each*)
1 cup Messina Hof Private Reserve Cabernet Sauvignon
*Wild Mushroom Duxelle*
2 tablespoons chopped garlic
2 tablespoons chopped shallots
6 tablespoons olive oil
6 tablespoons butter
1 cup chopped shiitake mushrooms
1 cup chopped portobello mushrooms
1 cup chopped button mushrooms
2 tablespoons minced fresh oregano
2 tablespoons minced fresh basil
4 cups Messina Hof Merlot
Salt and pepper to taste

1 sheet puff pastry
4 cups fresh spinach, steamed
2 eggs, beaten

Toss garlic cloves in 1 tablespoon oil; wrap in foil. Bake at 350° for 20–25 minutes or until browned. Meanwhile, cut each fillet into six square pieces. In a skillet, sear beef in remaining oil until browned on both sides. Add Cabernet; reduce until wine is almost gone (meat should be rare at this point).

For duxelle, in a saucepan, sauté garlic and shallots in oil for 2 minutes. Add the butter, mushrooms, oregano and basil; sauté 2 minutes longer. Add Merlot; cook over low heat until dry, stirring often. Season with salt and pepper.

Cut puff pastry sheet into 12 squares; top each square with one piece of meat, three garlic cloves, a spoonful of duxelle and a spoonful of steamed spinach. Wrap pastry around filling; place seam side down on a baking sheet. Brush with eggs. Bake at 350° for 15–20 minutes or until golden brown.

Serves 3

# Chicken Zitrone

2 boneless skinless chicken breast halves (4 to 6
    ounces *each*)
$1/4$ cup all-purpose flour
$1/4$ cup olive oil
2 tablespoons chopped garlic
6 water-packed artichoke hearts, drained
$1/3$ cup sliced fresh mushrooms
$1/4$ cup diced red bell pepper
3 tablespoons chopped fresh basil
2 tablespoons lemon juice
$1/2$ cup Messina Hof Chardonnay
2 tablespoons cold butter
Salt and pepper to taste

Dredge chicken in flour. In a skillet, heat oil; sauté chicken on both sides until browned. Add the garlic, artichokes, mushrooms and red pepper; continue to sauté. Add basil, lemon juice and wine; cook until reduced. Add butter, a tablespoon at a time, and whisk until incorporated. Season with salt and pepper.

Serves 2

# Chardonnay Chicken Pasta

*After spending a long day working in the wine cellar, we often choose pasta for a quick but filling dinner. This recipe is a great way to use leftover grilled chicken.*

8 ounces uncooked linguine
1/2 cup *each* chopped red, green and yellow bell peppers
1 tablespoon minced garlic
1/4 cup olive oil
1 can (2 1/4 ounces) sliced black olives, drained
1/4 cup chopped water-packed artichoke hearts, drained
2 grilled chicken breast halves, sliced
1/4 cup Messina Hof Chardonnay
Salt and pepper to taste
2 tablespoons crumbled feta cheese

Cook linguine according to package directions. Meanwhile, in a skillet, sauté the peppers and garlic in oil until tender. Stir in the olives, artichokes and chicken; sauté 2 minutes longer. Deglaze with wine; reduce by half. Season with salt and pepper. Drain linguine; toss with chicken mixture. Top with feta cheese.

Serves 2

*"Both of our families spent many hours around the family dining table or the kitchen stove sharing laughs, comforting woes and celebrating day-to-day victories."* —Merrill

# Inspiration from France and Germany

We took two trips to France, one in 1991 and again in 1994, and those years were real turning points in Messina Hof's growth.

In 1991, the Houston Club awarded our wines as Best of Show, and we went with an educational group to Burgundy. Attending classes at the University of Dijon during the morning and visiting the great wineries of Burgundy in the afternoon, we learned the intricacies of producing Pinot Noir and Chardonnay, which influenced our own winemaking style. Imagine being in the vineyard of Montrachet the day they are pruning and bringing back a cutting to graft in our vineyard in Halfway, Texas!

In 1994, we traveled with an educational group to Bordeaux. Our mornings were filled with academics of wine production in that region ... in the afternoons we visited the wineries, where we discussed winemaking philosophies with the winemakers ... and in the evenings we enjoyed fabulous meals of wine and food from the regions. What inspiration!

The second trip was my favorite because our son, Paul Mitchell, traveled with us, and because we went as a family to visit Hof and Messina while in Europe. In addition, this trip did more to shape the future of Messina Hof than anything else we had experienced.

In Germany, we savored great bratwurst roasted in open-fire ovens, poached veal rump with wine soup (wein stein), venison with lentil soup, veal chops with fried grape leaves, apple strudel and baked apples stuffed with mascarpone.

In Bordeaux, we dined each night at a different chateau, with the personal chef of the Mouton Rothschild estate as our caterer. Each dish featured wine as an ingredient, and every pairing was perfection. I realize now how important this trip was in planting memory seeds that inspired the passion revealed in each aspect of Messina Hof.

The French have a flair for fashion in food. My favorites were mandarin orange flower petals around a beautifully painted chocolate flower ... lemon cake with layers of lemon custard created in a cylindrical tower ... grilled foie gras with baked apples ... veal chops with mushrooms ... and pears poached in wine. At the end of every meal, a delightfully arranged board of local artisan cheeses was presented.

In my travel journal I wrote, "I think people buy wines because of the way they make you feel. St. Emillon makes you feel that you are part of the history of the village. It is quiet, closed and familial." This is the way Paul and I wanted Messina Hof to be experienced and remembered.

A culture is defined by the character of its people, the architecture in relationship to the region, its food, wine and art. European communities have evolved into a self-realized comfort. Each element fits naturally with the other and seems to be timeless. —*Merrill*

# Papa Paulo Texas Port and Pecan Tasties

*This dessert is one of our friend Karen Grampp's great pairings for our Papa Paulo Port.*

2 cups vanilla wafer crumbs
2 cups finely chopped Texas pecans
2 cups confectioners' sugar
5 tablespoons unsweetened cocoa
3 tablespoons light corn syrup
²∕₃ cup Messina Hof Papa Paulo Texas Port
Additional confectioners' sugar

In a mixing bowl, combine the wafer crumbs, pecans, confectioners' sugar and cocoa. Add corn syrup and wine; blend well (mixture will be sticky). Cover tightly and chill for 1 hour or until dough is easy to handle.

Drop teaspoonfuls of dough into a small bowl of confectioners' sugar, rolling them until coated. Place balls in a single layer in a pan or container. Cover tightly with plastic wrap to seal in the great flavor. Store in the refrigerator.

Makes about 8 dozen

# Chocolate Pâté

*Chocolate is an ideal pairing for port. In 1986, our wine and food experiments became our wine-based food line with jellies, mustards, port fudge sauce and port wine chocolate truffles. Each year, we added a new wine-based food product to the Messina Hof wine food line.*

1¹/₂ pounds semisweet chocolate, chopped
1³/₄ pounds butter, cubed
¹/₂ pound confectioners' sugar
¹/₂ cup Messina Hof Papa Paulo Texas Port
9 eggs, beaten

In the top of a double boiler, melt chocolate and butter. Whisk in confectioners' sugar and wine. Slowly add eggs, whisking constantly. Pour into buttered miniature loaf pans; cool. Store in the refrigerator. Slice like pâté to serve.

Serves 10

# Gingerbread

*For non-chocolate lovers (are there any out there?), try a piece of gingerbread with a glass of port, and you will be surprised what a great pairing it is!*

3 cups sifted whole-wheat flour
1 tablespoon ground cinnamon
1 teaspoon baking soda
1 teaspoon ground ginger
1 teaspoon ground cloves
$1/2$ teaspoon salt
1 cup packed brown sugar
1 cup vegetable oil
3 eggs, well beaten
1 cup sour milk
1 cup molasses

Sift together the flour, cinnamon, baking soda, ginger, cloves and salt; set aside. In a mixing bowl, combine the brown sugar, oil, eggs, milk and molasses; beat until blended. Beat in the dry ingredients. Pour into a greased and floured 13-inch x 9-inch x 2-inch baking pan. Bake at 350° for 35–45 minutes or until firm to the touch.

Serves 8

# Fruit Cocktail Cake

2 cups all-purpose flour

1$\frac{1}{2}$ cups sugar

2 teaspoons baking soda

2 eggs, well beaten

1 cup diced mixed fruit (strawberries, pineapple, peaches, apricots)

$\frac{1}{2}$ cup packed brown sugar

*Icing*

1 cup sugar

1 cup milk

2 tablespoons butter

$\frac{1}{2}$ cup flaked coconut

$\frac{1}{2}$ cup chopped pecans

1 teaspoon vanilla extract

Sift flour, sugar and baking soda three times into a large mixing bowl. Add eggs and fruit; mix well. Pour into a greased and floured loaf pan. Sprinkle brown sugar over batter. Bake at 350° for 30–40 minutes. In a saucepan over medium heat, cook and stir the sugar, milk and butter until thickened. Stir in coconut, pecans and vanilla. Ice the cake while still hot.

Serves 8-10

# Orange Date Cake

*This make-ahead cake stores nicely and tastes even better after freezing.*

1 teaspoon baking soda
1¼ cups buttermilk
1 cup butter, softened
4 cups sugar, *divided*
4 cups all-purpose flour
4 eggs
½ pound chopped dates
1 cup chopped pecans
4 teaspoons orange zest, *divided*
1 teaspoon vanilla extract
1 cup fresh orange juice

*"The family table has been the grounding root that binds families for generations. The kitchen and dining room tables allow families the time to communicate. It is a time of laughter and sharing. It is a time to share the history of our forefathers, the science of cooking, the grace of conversation and understanding of family values."* —Merrill

Dissolve baking soda in buttermilk. In a large mixing bowl, cream butter and 2 cups sugar. Beat in flour and eggs. Add baking soda mixture, dates, pecans, 2 teaspoons orange zest and vanilla. Pour into a large tube pan. Bake at 325° for 1¼ hours.

In a saucepan, combine the orange juice and remaining sugar and orange zest; heat until sugar is dissolved (do not boil). When cake is done, remove from the oven. With a sharp knife, make holes all over the top of the cake, to a depth of halfway to two-thirds into the cake. Pour orange mixture into holes. Leave cake in pan overnight. Let stand for 2 days before cutting.

Serves 12

# Port and Cream Freeze

3 scoops (8 ounces *each*) vanilla ice cream
¹/₂ cup milk
¹/₂ cup Messina Hof Papa Paulo Port
Chocolate shavings

Place the ice cream, milk and wine in a blender; cover and process until blended. Pour into chilled glasses; sprinkle with chocolate shavings. Serve immediately. Beverage will have the consistency of a milk shake; to make it thicker, reduce the milk.

Serves 2

# Tawny Port Latte

1 tablespoon Messina Hof Tawny Port
1 shot brewed espresso
³/₄ cup steamed milk
³/₄ cup half-and-half cream

Pour wine into a cappuccino mug; add espresso (stirring is not necessary, as mixture will blend when poured). Blend milk and cream; add to wine and espresso mixture according to cappuccino maker instructions.

**For Tawny Port Cappuccino:** Froth blended milk and cream according to cappuccino maker instructions and add to wine and espresso mixture. Spoon extra froth over beverage for presentation.

Serves 1

# Mama Rosa's Summer Cooler

1 bottle Messina Hof Mama Rosa Rosé
1 tablespoon honey
3 strawberries, hulled and halved
2 sprigs fresh mint

Pour the wine into a carafe or clear pitcher. Stir in honey until dissolved; add strawberries and mint. Refrigerate for 3 hours or overnight. Strain; discard berries and mint. Serve over cracked ice with a fresh sprig of mint for garnish.

Serves 2

# Fireside Mulled Wine

1 bottle Messina Hof Shiraz
1½ cups water *or* brewed green tea
½ cup raw *or* brown sugar
8 whole cloves
1 cinnamon stick
¼ teaspoon grated nutmeg
Pinch allspice

Place all ingredients in a saucepan; warm over low heat (do not boil). Steep for 30 minutes. Strain and discard cloves and cinnamon; serve in mugs.

**For Papa Paulo Port Mulled Wine:** Substitute port for the shiraz, reduce the water to ¾ cup and reduce the sugar to ¼ cup (port is already sweet). Add ½ teaspoon orange zest if desired. This makes a bolder mulled wine for those really cold nights.

Serves 2-3

*"Water separates people and wine brings people together."* —Paul

# Keep the Love Growing

What love story would be complete without a little romance? The most popular Cooking Parties turned out to be a real surprise—couples and singles of all ages signed up for "Aphrodisiacs." Some tips shared at the event were:

- Prepare for your romantic dinner well in advance, so you have little to do at the last minute and can enjoy the evening with your significant other.
- If you have children, plan a late dinner or find an outside sitter.
- Chill the wine (if white).
- Select a small table, if possible, so your knees will touch when seated.
- If you have a fireplace, place the table in front of a blazing fire for added ambience.
- Pull out your best china, crystal and silverware and your finest tablecloth, preferably in a light color (peach or rose is best).
- Place candles and flowers on the table to evoke pleasurable aromas and thoughts. Stay away from highly scented flowers or candles, so you don't cover up the inviting aromas of your meal.
- Dim the lights and put on soothing background music.
- Make sure the answering machine is on and in silent mode.

# Carrot-Mango Chutney

*Carrots are believed to be a stimulant. They were used by early Middle Eastern royalty to aid in seduction.*

6 tablespoons olive oil
1 cup diced peeled carrots
1 cup diced peeled mango
2 tablespoons diced shallots
2 tablespoons chopped garlic
2 tablespoons chopped chives
1/2 cup Messina Hof Gewürztraminer
1/2 cup apple cider vinegar
1/4 cup packed brown sugar

Heat oil in a saucepan. Add carrots and cook until browned, being careful not to burn. Add mango, shallots and garlic; cook until shallots become translucent. Stir in the remaining ingredients; simmer until mixture becomes slightly thickened. Taste and adjust sweetness and seasoning if needed.

Makes 4 cups

# Messina Hof Mustard Vinaigrette Salad

*Almonds have been a symbol of fertility throughout the ages; the aroma is thought to induce passion. Mustard is believed to stimulate the sexual glands and increase desire.*

*Roasted Tomatoes*
3 plum tomatoes, cored and halved
4 tablespoons olive oil
¼ cup chopped fresh basil
1 tablespoon chopped garlic
1 tablespoon sugar
Salt and pepper to taste
*Vinaigrette*
3 tablespoons Messina Hof Pinot Grigio
2 tablespoons Messina Hof Chardonnay
2 tablespoons Dijon mustard
2 tablespoons white vinegar
1 tablespoon chopped garlic
1½ tablespoons chopped fresh basil
1½ tablespoons chopped fresh oregano
1½ cups vegetable oil
*Salad*
3 cups mixed salad greens
6 spears asparagus, blanched
¼ cup almonds, toasted

In a bowl, combine the tomatoes, olive oil, basil, garlic, sugar, salt and pepper. Transfer to a baking dish. Bake, uncovered, at 300° for 1 hour.

For vinaigrette, place the wines, mustard, vinegar, garlic, basil and oregano in a blender. With blender running, slowly drizzle in vegetable oil, blending until incorporated. Toss greens with desired amount of vinaigrette; place on plates. Top with roasted tomatoes, asparagus and almonds. Refrigerate remaining vinaigrette.

## Serves 2

*"I will never forget two things that Paul told me about marriage: We did not need a best man or woman, because in life we would be each other's best; and that life is made of a library of memories. The objective is to fill the library with many great memories that will carry us through the difficult times." —Merrill*

# Pair of Ports Pie

*The Aztecs referred to chocolate as "nourishment of the gods."*

4 cups finely crushed chocolate cookies
$^1/_2$ cup butter, melted
*Chocolate Mousse Layer*
12 ounces semisweet chocolate, chopped
$^1/_2$ cup butter
3 tablespoons Messina Hof Papa Paulo Port
8 egg yolks
4 tablespoons sugar, *divided*
$^3/_4$ cup heavy whipping cream
2 tablespoons sour cream
2 egg whites
*White Chocolate Mousse Layer*
9 ounces white chocolate, chopped
2$^1/_2$ cups heavy whipping cream, *divided*
3 tablespoons Messina Hof Ivory Ports of Call
3 egg yolks
2$^1/_2$ tablespoons sugar, *divided*
2 egg whites

Combine the cookie crumbs and melted butter; press onto the bottom of a 9-inch springform pan. Set aside.

In a double boiler, melt semisweet chocolate and butter; add wine. In a mixing bowl, whip egg yolks and 3 tablespoons sugar until creamy. Add chocolate mixture. Cool.

In another bowl, whip cream and sour cream until stiff peaks form. Fold into chocolate mixture. Whip egg whites and remaining sugar until stiff peaks form; fold into chocolate mixture. Pour over prepared crust. Freeze for 20 minutes.

In a double boiler, melt white chocolate with 3 tablespoons cream; add wine. In a mixing bowl, whip egg yolks and 1½ tablespoons sugar until creamy. Whisk in chocolate mixture. Whip the remaining cream until stiff peaks form; fold into chocolate mixture. Whip egg whites and remaining sugar until stiff peaks form; fold into chocolate mixture. Pour over semisweet mousse layer. Freeze overnight.

Serves 12

# Story Came Full Circle

Our son's flair for cooking was evident early when he'd prepare dinner for us on days I was working late. Paul Mitchell also has a great palate, which was honed in tastings with his father. Though Paul VII was the next winemaker of the family, he had a love of the military and a passion for the Marine Corps that led him to the U.S. Naval Academy in Annapolis, Maryland.

On one of our many trips to visit him, we took a morning stroll near the docks and discovered a statue of Alex Haley, the author of *Roots*. The Kunta Kinte-Alex Haley Memorial commemorates the place of arrival of Alex Haley's African ancestor, a pioneer in his own day, leading his people to a new world and a new life. Our story had come full circle. Messina Hof was inspired by a man from Annapolis, where Paul VII graduated from the Naval Academy in 2005.

On May 25, 2005, just prior to his Senior Ball at the academy, Paul VII put on his Marine Corps apron and created a beautiful meal for his new love, Karen. Ten months later, they married. What an ironic tale. A Northern man came to Texas and found the love of his life in a Texas woman ... our Texas son found the love of his life

in a Northern woman.

The meal he served included a Smoked Salmon Rose, Crawfish Crab Cakes and Chicken Marsala, with Apple Crisp for dessert. —*Merrill*

# Smoked Salmon Rose

1 slice pumpernickel bread
2 tablespoons sour cream
4 ounces smoked salmon, sliced
2 tablespoons capers
2 tablespoons minced red onion
1 hard-boiled egg, finely chopped
1 teaspoon caviar

Cut the slice of pumpernickel into a round about the size of a doughnut. Place on a plate and spread with sour cream. Roll salmon slices into the shape of a rose; place over sour cream. Garnish with capers, onion, egg and caviar.

Makes 1 rose

# Crawfish Crab Cakes

*You can make these crab cakes on their own, or serve them with one or both of the sauces for a pretty presentation.*

*Lemon-Chive Beurre Blanc*
1 quart heavy cream
2 cups white wine
1 cup lemon juice
2 teaspoons lemon zest
2 whole cloves
2 bay leaves
1 pound cold butter
1 cup chopped fresh chives
*Roasted Pepper Coulis*
2 cups chicken stock
$1/2$ cup white wine
2 roasted red peppers
1 teaspoon chopped leek
1 teaspoon chopped shallot
Salt and pepper to taste
*Crab Cakes*
$3/4$ pound lump crabmeat
$1/2$ pound cooked crawfish tails
$1 1/4$ cups breadcrumbs
$1/2$ cup mayonnaise
1 egg, beaten

$1/4$ cup diced red bell pepper
$2 1/2$ tablespoons diced red onion
$1/2$ tablespoon lemon juice
$1/2$ tablespoon Worcestershire sauce
$1/2$ tablespoon Dijon mustard
$1/2$ teaspoon cayenne pepper
$1/2$ teaspoon minced garlic
$1/4$ teaspoon celery seed
$1/4$ teaspoon salt
White pepper to taste

For beurre blanc, combine the cream, wine, lemon juice and zest, cloves and bay leaves in a saucepan. Reduce by one-third. Add butter, a little at a time, until incorporated. Discard cloves and bay leaves. Stir chives into sauce; keep warm.

For coulis, combine the stock, wine, red peppers, leek and shallot in another saucepan. Simmer for about 20 minutes. Purée; season with salt and pepper.

In a large bowl, mix all crab cake ingredients until well combined. Form into patties, about 2-3 inches in diameter. Sauté in butter until golden brown. Serve with beurre blanc and coulis.

Makes about 1 dozen

# Bonarrigo Chicken Marsala

2 boneless skinless chicken breasts (8 ounces *each*)
1/2 cup all-purpose flour
1/4 cup olive oil
3 tablespoons chopped garlic
1 cup sliced fresh mushrooms
3 tablespoons chopped fresh parsley
1/2 cup Messina Hof Private Reserve Papa Paulo Port
1/4 cup chicken stock
3 tablespoons butter
Salt and pepper to taste

Dredge chicken in flour. In a skillet, heat oil; sauté chicken until browned on both sides. Add garlic; sauté for 2 minutes. Add mushrooms, parsley, wine and stock. Simmer until chicken juices run clear. Add butter; season with salt and pepper.

*Serves 2*

# Paul's Apple Crisp

6 apples, peeled and thinly sliced
3 to 4 tablespoons brown sugar
1/2 to 1 teaspoon ground cinnamon
3/4 cup sugar
1/2 cup rolled oats
1/4 cup all-purpose flour
1/4 cup cold butter
Vanilla ice cream

Place the apples in a greased 13-inch x 9-inch x 2-inch baking dish. Combine brown sugar and cinnamon; sprinkle over apples. For topping, combine the sugar, oats and flour in a bowl; cut in butter until mixture is crumbly (if mixture is too dry, add more butter). Sprinkle over apples, making sure apples are covered (make more topping if needed). Bake at 375° for 40 minutes. Serve warm with vanilla ice cream.

*Serves 8*

# A Memorable Start to a New Life Together

After 20 years of planning romantic weddings and receptions for others, I was thrilled to produce one for my own son. Paul and I celebrated the marriage of our son, Second Lieutenant Paul M. Bonarrigo, to Karen Pietruszka on March 18, 2006.

Paul and Karen selected an outdoor ceremony at the Living Waterfall Garden Gazebo, situated in a meadow between the vineyard and the lake. This particular vineyard was significant, as it was planted the same year Paul was born.

Following the nuptials, the bride and groom joined their guests in the Vintage House Vineyard Room for a sunset reception overlooking the vineyard. Tables were dressed in Marine Corps colored satin linens, gold-leaf candles were clustered on beds of rose petals, and frames held photos of memories the couple had already shared.

Dinner featured grilled petit fillets, salmon with smoked bacon and caramelized onions, wild mushroom ravioli and duck breast with Papa Paulo Port demi-glace. Fresh herbs and seasonal vegetables came from the vineyard gardens. Guests could also enjoy a chocolate fountain with fruit and biscotti for dipping. (Paul and Karen enjoy baking these Italian cookies together.)

For the newlyweds, their most memorable moment was exchanging personal vows from the heart, and the private walk they took through the woods and around the lake to the reception. They said they would always remember that tender moment as they began their walk in life together.

For my husband and me, it was the best of times, sharing the fulfillment of our dreams and our son's dreams together where it all began—the vineyard.

God bless the Texas wine industry and all of those who have been part of our lives. This is the first chapter of the rest of our lives together. We look forward to the plan the Lord has for us. Keep your hearts open so you may hear His direction. —*Merrill*

*"Trust in the Lord and do good; dwell in the land and enjoy safe pasture. Delight yourself in the Lord and He will give you the desires of your heart." Psalm 37:3-4 (NIV)*

159

# Appendix

Most people purchase wine based on style. It is difficult to know by looking at most labels what style the wine might be. Messina Hof developed a color-coding system to help you.

Four colors represent the different styles of wines we produce. Dry white wines—like Sauvignon Blanc, Pinot Grigio and Chardonnay—have a sapphire blue stripe. This symbolizes the crisp, refreshing, distinctive character of dry wines. Fruity wines with some sweetness—like Chenin Blanc, Riesling or Gewürztraminer—are graced by an emerald green stripe to express the fresh, youthful character of these wines. Our red wines are rich, robust and smooth on the palate; they have a burgundy stripe. And our dessert wines that are very sweet are denoted with a black stripe.

In case you forget, there is a color legend on the label as well. With the color system, picking the right wine is a snap.

For more information on our wines and winery, visit our Web site at *messinahof.com*.

Green striped labels — semisweet and fruity wines
Blue striped labels — dry white wines
Burgundy striped labels — dry red wines
Black striped labels — sweet dessert wines

## White Wines

### Chardonnay

Chardonnay stands above all white wines as the most noble of grapes. It can be found predominantly in regions of France that produce Chablis, Pouilly-Fuissé, Montrachet and Champagne. Messina Hof's Chardonnay is pure and full-bodied. This is developed through its brief aging in French oak, producing a heavy, velvety aroma and taste. We have three types:

Private Reserve Chardonnay, the best of the vintage, has the longest exposure to oak in fermentation and aging.

Barrel Reserve Chardonnay is also barrel fermented and aged, but it spends less time in oak and has more fruit flavors.

Un-oaked Chardonnay is the most fruitful of the selections with light oak aging.

### Sauvignon Blanc

The primary grape of the Loire Valley and the Graves districts of Bordeaux, Sauvignon Blanc traditionally produces a crisp, dry white wine. Messina Hof's Sauvignon Blanc is blended in the Bordeaux style with Sémillon and aged in French oak barrels. Its natural flavors of melon and fig are enhanced by wonderful floral and herbal aromas.

## Pinot Grigio

Also known as Pinot Gris, Pinot Grigio is a traditional grape of Italy. It has gained great notoriety as a crisp, refreshing, dry white wine similar to Sauvignon Blanc. Pinot Grigio has mellow tropical fruit, melon and fig characteristics in addition to a wonderfully crisp citrus finish. It creates a luscious and very food-friendly wine.

## Chenin Blanc

Chenin Blanc is an excellent light white wine that is the predominant white varietal of the French regions of Touraine and Anjou. Messina Hof's Chenin Blanc is a fresh, pale and early maturing wine of considerable finesse and character. It has balanced acidity and ripened rose petal aromas, which give hint to its sweet, fruity nature.

Fermented cold—using a Northern Italian yeast strain—and bottled cold, the wine retains its natural carbon dioxide, which creates a lively mouthfeel.

## Riesling

The Riesling grape, also known as White Riesling, originates from Germany's most famous vineyards, spectacularly situated on one of the steepest Rheingau hillsides. According to legend, Emperor Charlemagne first ordered the vines planted on this slope. Yellow when ripe, the grape is known for its flowery aroma and sweet nectar flavors.

Messina Hof's Riesling is semi-dry with rich fruit overtones, especially Granny Smith apples.

Our Angel Late Harvest Riesling is a dessert wine made from grapes allowed to mature on the vine 2 weeks after the other grapes are harvested.

## Gewürztraminer

Originating from the noble grape of Germany and Alsace, France, Gewürztraminer is a semi-dry, light white wine with intense and distinctive herbal aromas, plus distinguishable characteristics of sweet and spicy. The nose is reminiscent of spices such as ginger and allspice.

## Muscat Canelli

Muscat Canelli originates in Northern Italy and is famous for its perfumed floral character ... so much so that it is used in perfume production in France. It lends itself to semi-dry table wines as well as dessert wines like Messina Hof's Glory Late Harvest Muscat Canelli and Ivory Ports of Call.

Our Muscat Canelli is very characteristic of the Italian varietal; our most aromatic wine, it is refreshingly sweet with floral scents and ripe apricot flavors.

Ivory Ports of Call is a rich blend of Glory Late Harvest Muscat Canelli and barrel-fermented Sauvignon Blanc. Ivory is a light port with medium to heavy body and long aftertaste of sweet grapefruit and green melon flavors.

## Blush

In the early 1980s, Rosé was reintroduced under the new name of Blush. Rosé wines were popular before World War II but lost popularity in the United States in favor of German white wines.

Blush is made from Zinfandel, Cabernet Sauvignon, Ruby Cabernet, Merlot and Pinot Noir grapes, which are pressed immediately at harvest to remove the skins; they are pressed only until sufficient pink color is achieved. The resulting wine is fresh, fruity and bottled quickly to retain the effervescence of youth.

Mama Rosa Rosé and White Zinfandel are Messina Hof's Blush wines.

# Red Wines

### Shiraz

Tradition has it that Shiraz is named for the area of the grape's origin—Shiraz, Iran. The Australians preserved the original name while the French changed it to Syrah. Shiraz has a rich color of ruby red to dark garnet with a nose of ripe plums, black currants, and hints of wood and molasses.

Texas Shiraz is characteristically rich and jammy, with currant flavors, and hints of blackberry and bourbon in the finish. Soft tannins from new oak nicely balance the fruit and give the wine a bold structure.

## Pinot Noir

Pinot Noir is the red grape of Burgundy, France. It produces wines that are lighter in body with heavy fruit flavors such as cherry and blackberry.

The Messina Hof Barrel Reserve Pinot Noir is crafted in true French Burgundian style. Rich, warm wood scents layered with flavors of winterberries develop during aging in small French oak casks.

Our Private Reserve Pinot Noir, aged for 2 years in oak, has robust flavor and velvety texture. Oak aging adds complexity of vanilla, nutmeg and toast flavors to the wine.

## Cabernet Sauvignon

Originating from the Medoc region of France, Cabernet Sauvignon is considered one of the world's best red grapes, producing a long-lived, slow-maturing wine. Aged in American oak, Cabernet Sauvignon is a rich, mellow wine of finesse and charm.

Messina Hof produces a Private Reserve Cabernet Sauvignon from the oldest Cabernet Sauvignon vines and blended with Merlot.

The Barrel Reserve Cabernet Sauvignon is also a blend of Merlot and Cabernet Sauvignon, but it isn't aged as long as the Private Reserve.

## Zinfandel

Also known as Primitivo, Zinfandel is a rich red grape varietal producing a dark, ruby-red wine best known for its spicy fruit. It is the wine most similar to Chianti.

Messina Hof's Barrel Reserve Zinfandel has a hearty spice character with ripe berries.

The Private Reserve Zinfandel is aged 2 years in oak, 1 year in French oak and then 1 year in American oak, enhancing the earthy character in the wine.

## Merlot

In recent years, Merlot has come into its own as a varietal that is peppery and smoky with blackberry and cherry overtones. The Merlot grape also provides the soft, velvety texture to the great Cabernet Sauvignons and French Bordeaux. Soft and silky, it can produce wines of rich and spicy fruit.

Merlot is a region-specific grape, meaning that its aromas and flavors change depending on the areas in which it is planted, more so than other varieties.

Messina Hof's Merlot is a dry red that is rich, spicy and robust in flavor. It is full-bodied and supple with good structure.

## Cabernet Franc

Called the "father of grapes," Cabernet Franc can boast a lineage that produced Cabernet Sauvignon and Sauvignon Blanc. Used primarily as a blender for Cabernet Sauvignon and Merlot in Bordeaux-style wines, Cabernet Franc has become a popular varietal in its own right. An earthiness to the wine is layered with tobacco and hints of raspberry.

## Ruby Port

Port originated as "Porto" from Portugal centuries ago. Porto is made from red wine, and when the wine is ready to be aged in the barrel, brandy is added to stop the fermentation process. While the port is in the barrel, the brandy and wine marry, creating the luscious chocolate and cherry flavors for which port is known. Port should be served at room temperature to bring out these unique flavors.

Messina Hof's Port is unique in that no brandy is added. The Lenoir grape harvested from our estate vineyards achieves high sugar levels. We add a special yeast, which allows the wine to ferment slowly to the 19–20% alcohol level naturally. This produces a much smoother, more mellow wine early.

Our Papa Paulo Port is aged in small oak casks and emits chocolate and cherry aromas.

# Recipe Index

# Acknowledgments

L ife is not about what we do. It is about the people with whom we share our time. This book would not have been possible without the wonderful people who helped create it.

We thank the Lord for the privilege of stewarding Messina Hof. Thank you to all our family, friends and employees who have helped us since 1977. Special thanks to Ken Rudd, Fred and Karen Grampp, Barb and Joe Szumanski, Jeff Matthews and Kevin Fotorny.

We wish to thank Mark Davis, who produced the beautiful photographs of the Messina Hof vineyards, winery, kitchen garden, restaurant and many striking food photographs. Our thanks also go to Chandler Arden, Rob Camper, Russell James and Anne Perry for their photographic contributions.

Finally, we are grateful to Publisher Rue Judd, Designer Isabel Lasater Hernandez, Editor Kristine Krueger and the entire staff at Bright Sky Press.